WAITING WITH GOD

FOR HIS GOOD GIFTS OF MARRIAGE & SEX

A TRUE LOVE STORY BY STEPHEN & REBECCA ANTHONY

Copyright © 2014 by Stephen and Rebecca Anthony

All rights reserved. No portion of this book may be reproduced, stored in a retrieval system, or transmitted in any form or by any means—electronic, mechanical, photocopy, recording, scanning, or other—except for brief quotations in critical reviews or articles, without the prior written permission of the author.

Unless otherwise noted, Scripture quotations are taken from *The Holy Bible, New International Version*®, NIV® Copyright © 1973, 1978, 1984, 2011 by Biblica, Inc.® Used by permission. All rights reserved worldwide.

Scripture taken from *The Message*. Copyright © 1993, 1994, 1995, 1996, 2000, 2001, 2002. Used by permission of NavPress Publishing Group.

Cover Design: Jared Fuller
Cover Illustration: Shutterstock

A portion of the profits from this book will be sent to ministries that encourage sexual purity and to organizations working to end sex trafficking and slavery.

DEDICATION

This book is lovingly dedicated to the Anthony and Fuller families—past, present, and future.

Thanks to:

Our Creator—for being our matchmaker and for giving us such a beautiful love story.

Our family and friends—for your encouragement and support over the years. You have believed in us, and we are forever grateful for your love.

The "Women Writing for a Change" group, 2012—for enthusiastically encouraging me (Rebecca) to "keep writing."

Deerfoot Lodge—a Christian wilderness camp for boys in the Adirondack Mountains of upstate New York. Deerfoot was instrumental in my (Stephen's) development spiritually, emotionally, mentally, and physically.

Klemmer—a tool that God used to help me (Stephen) push through obstacles so that I could be more successful in my career, in love, and in the challenge of writing this book.

Jared—for being our graphic designer extraordinaire. We are grateful for your generosity, patience, and creativity.

The counselors who have walked beside us over the years. We are forever grateful for the healing that came as we sat with you.

A special thank-you to the following who have offered editing help:

Denise—for prayerfully and thoughtfully doing the first, and many additional, edits on this book. Thank you for wholeheartedly believing that ours is a story that needs to be told.

Chris—for your honest, wise, and helpful feedback and suggestions.

Nadine—for asking thought-provoking questions that helped us go deeper and be more real.

Huddy and Mary—for bringing this project to completion with such wisdom and care.

Beyond Sight

A river of salty tears
Let me sail upon
Far from trifles and tragedies
Yet, the moisture digs and etches

Melting clay hard rocks of stubble
Tender, grey-green shoots
Poke and prod birthing
Announcing roots beyond the eyes

Process of death and life
Open-handed soldiers laying down weapons
Picking up white banners saying
Let come, what comes

Face reflected in the water
Lined by allowing
Entrance to friends and betrayers
Disappointed because hope made a promise

Unfulfilled waiting, watching
Remembrance of flowers
Grants acceptance of rain
Standing firm in ridiculous trust

That beneath the grass are roots
Behind the clouds is sun
Folded in the stocking is a present
Inside the twinkling eye is love

(Wait, Trust, Hope, Surrender. Amen.)

By: Shelley Pearson

Contents

Intro: What's your deepest desire? 1

Chapter 1: Why am I waiting? 3

Chapter 2: Something is missing 25

Chapter 3: He'll be worth the wait 41

Chapter 4: I will be dating my future husband by my 35th birthday 53

Chapter 5: What if your future husband doesn't live in Seattle? 63

Chapter 6: I want to marry you 91

Chapter 7: I could never live in such a small town 99

Chapter 8: Don't come back 'til you find yourself 105

Chapter 9: He is all I've ever hoped for, for you! 113

Chapter 10: It doesn't matter what you like; it's about what she likes! 117

Chapter 11: Yes! 121

Chapter 12: It's a reminder of God's faithfulness............ 129

Chapter 13: I'd rather move to the desert if God is inviting me there, than live in lush meadows of my own choosing..................... 135

Chapter 14: I want to make out with him 24-7.............. 143

Chapter 15: How sweet it is to be loved by you............. 151

Chapter 16: Yeah baby, that's what I'm talking about.... 163

Chapter 17: Nothing is impossible for Me...................... 169

Chapter 18: His name means "gift from God" 187

Chapter 19: Sex is fun and pleasurable 201

Epilogue: Invitations.. 206

INTRODUCTION

What's your deepest desire?

We were both virgins when we got married. Stephen was thirty-nine and I was thirty-five. As we shared parts of the story of how we met, we kept getting feedback like, "Wow, that's an amazing love story . . . you need to write that down." We both had always wanted to write a book. Plus, we loved the idea of someday, for Christmas, giving our kids a hard copy of our book, with all the details of our journey in finding each other. We also had a deep desire to encourage others with the truth: *God cares about the well-being of your love life, even more than you do.*

We imagine that many of the readers who find our book will share our faith in God. However, we want to extend a warm invitation to those of you who practice other faiths and who express your spirituality differently than us. We pray that wherever you are in your spiritual journey, you would be open to the Divine speaking to you.

As you read our story—a story of waiting, struggle, joy, and God's faithfulness—may you be encouraged and challenged in the choices you make regarding your sexuality. We pray that you will be infused with the courage to wait and hope for what *your* heart most longs for.

If you are single, desiring marriage, know that Jesus hears the cries of your heart. We pray that God would unite you with a godly mate, in His best and most loving timing for you both. If you don't desire marriage, or if you're already married, we pray you would discover what you are most passionate about pursuing during this season of your life, and that you too would be inspired to wait with God for His very best for you. Our hope is that no matter your age, faith practice, or relationship status, you would experience greater love, joy, peace, and guidance during this season of your life.

For Reflection:

1. What does your heart most long for?
2. Do you feel stuck in pursuing your dreams? If so, ask the Divine to reveal to you any false messages you may believe about yourself. Ask God to write His truth on your heart.

CHAPTER 1

Why am I waiting?

Rebecca Reflects:

The first ten years of my life were spent in the country, in Rogue River, Oregon. I have precious memories of my parents reading Laura Ingalls Wilder's Little House books and C. S. Lewis's Chronicles of Narnia series to me before bed (this must be where I got my love for reading in bed). I also enjoyed baking my own little whole grain loaf of bread for my dad (with my mom's loving assistance), picking roses and wildflowers from our garden, frequenting the library, performing puppet shows and plays for my two younger brothers, and creating homemade greeting cards, which I sold to our neighbors.

During these early years I felt completely secure in the fact that my parents deeply loved me and enjoyed spending time with me. Sadly, though, I don't have memories of my parents verbally appreciating each other, or leaning in for a gentle hug or kiss. Even though it was subtle, I could feel the underlying tension between them.

When I was ten years old, things drastically changed. The day after my tenth birthday, my mom told my two younger brothers and me that we needed to quickly go to Southern California to visit our Grandpa (who we affectionately called "Daddy Pop"). My mom told us he was sick. Dad wouldn't be able to come because he couldn't get time off work. We piled into our 1975 orange VW camper, oblivious to the fact that our mom was bringing boxes full of our clothes and our pots and pans. On the drive, our van started sputtering and losing power. When my mom pulled over, she discovered that the butane tank had caught on fire. We quickly evacuated the van. I didn't have time to grab my new polka-dot bikini, which I had just received the day before for my tenth birthday. I also didn't have time to grab my white strappy sandals. I still remember how brutally hot the pavement had been that day. The way I remembered this event was that there had been a huge explosion, the kind you would witness in a blockbuster action movie. The more accurate reality, though, is that our van burned to the ground like a G.I. Joe toy being torched by a pyromaniacal kid. Our personal items were all burned and unsalvageable.

My dad had been verbally abusive toward my mom in their marriage, calling her degrading names. For a few years he had also, during rageful fits, turned physically violent toward my mother. Once he started verbally lashing out at one of my brothers, she decided she needed to protect us and leave.

Several months after we arrived in Southern California, my dad moved there to be closer to us. My mom (who had always loved being devoted to us kids 24-7) now had to start working two jobs outside the home. My parents divorced, my brothers and I moved into a tiny rental apartment with our mom, and I started public school after having been homeschooled. The quiet days of peacefully playing in a spacious and beautifully kept garden in the country, with my loving mom close by, were gone. My world now felt fast paced and confusing. I didn't see the full picture then, and I blamed my mom 100 percent for the divorce. My heart was full of anger toward her, and I often screamed, "I hope you know that you've ruined all of our lives!" It wasn't fair or accurate to put all the blame on my mom for the divorce, but I did.

My mom's dream of being married and getting to be a full-time mom was shattered. She now had to divide her time between us kids and working full time. Casseroles of brown rice and vegetables from our garden, and homemade strawberry ice cream, now had to be replaced with the occasional frozen pizza.

My mom was only thirty-three when my parents divorced. I was furious when she eventually started dating other men. I desperately wanted her and my dad to reconcile. I began to pray fervently that God would bring my parents back together. I continued praying for this miracle for the next eighteen years. I stopped praying after eighteen years because this is when my dad married my stepmom. I wanted to be happy for my dad, because he seemed excited to marry her, but I was devastated that God didn't answer my prayers. My parents, though, have since told me that they believe God did answer my prayers for reconciliation. They are now at peace with each other, and also with God and themselves. I've realized that it's tempting for me to try to control God and expect Him to answer my requests *my* way.

Getting back to when I was ten, this is also when I had a personal encounter with God for the first time. As a child, I had always religiously prayed before bed, "Now I lay me down to sleep, I pray the Lord my soul to keep. If I should die before I wake, I pray the Lord my soul to take." When I prayed, I was full of fear. I was not convinced that God heard me. I pleaded for God's attention and often begged Him to keep my family and me safe from bad things happening to us. After my parents' divorce, I lived with my mom and brothers, and we'd visit my dad on the weekends. My dad seemed somewhat restless, but something was definitely different. He didn't get as angry as quickly as he used to, and he seemed to be calmer. One day, I curiously asked him who he'd been hanging out with. He said, "Jesus Christ." I thought if Jesus was helping my dad feel happier and more at peace, then I too wanted to meet Him.

Two months later, during that tenth year, I was baptized in our church's baptismal Jacuzzi tub. I wore cute little pink shorts and a big yellow shirt with surfboards on it. Our pastor handed me the microphone and asked me to share why I wanted to get baptized. I shared that I loved having Jesus as my best friend and I wanted Him to be in my heart forever. As I was dunked, the water felt cool and refreshing against my skin. When I came up out of the water, someone on the church staff took a picture of me. I have regretfully misplaced this picture, but I do remember that in it my smile is huge. After each baptism, everyone cheered. We sang songs telling God how much we loved Him and how grateful we were to know lasting peace, no matter what circumstances came. It felt like one big party. I still look back on my baptism as one of *the* most celebratory days of my life. I felt alive and grounded in God's loving support toward me. It was like I was a waterfall, and God's love was gushing forth from me, spilling onto everyone I came in contact with. Saying yes to Jesus being my Savior filled me with joy, contentment, and love like I had never known. Having a loving God I could always talk with, no matter the time of day, and no matter how chaotic my home life became, was a huge source of security in the years to come.

In the fifth grade I started public school for the first time. I loved to read and had a vivid and creative imagination. Even though my grades were excellent, and my teacher told me I had amazing study skills and motivation, I still felt my math skills were lacking. Overall, I felt academically behind. I didn't feel smart enough to do the work assigned to me, and I also was shy and lacking in confidence with my classmates. One day during P.E. class, we were playing basketball, and one of my classmates, a short boy with bright red hair and freckles covering his round face, yelled at me, "F*** you!" I fearfully yelled back, "No!" All my classmates laughed at me for my awkward reaction. I thought he said "F*** you" because he wanted to have sex with me. This memory reminds me that I was an innocent and confused child when it came to things regarding sex and sexuality.

The first time I noticed being behind and left out regarding my love life happened in sixth grade. Two neighborhood girls and I were at a park sitting on the swings, chatting about our days at school. The conversation quickly turned to boys. They both beamed as they shared about the cute boys in class who liked them. One of my friends talked about how fun it was to kiss boys, and the other was giddy sharing about being asked out on a date to see a movie with the boy who liked her. I sat in silence as they talked. No cute boy liked me. No cute boy had asked me out on a date or kissed me. It felt painful to have absolutely nothing to add to the conversation. This scenario became familiar. Throughout high school and college, I would listen as girlfriends would gush about the joys of getting asked out to a school dance or about getting kissed for the first time. I tried my best to be supportive, but I often felt jealous. I felt forgotten by the male population, and by God Himself for never helping my crushes like me back.

When I was in the seventh grade, my mom and I continued to have a tense relationship, and I begged her to let me live with my dad. I thought living with him would be easier because he wasn't dating anyone and he also wanted to reconcile with my mom.

My mom continued to date, and my parents did not reconcile. I did not agree with some of her dating choices. However, I was so full of anger and resentment over my parents' divorce and lack of reconciliation that I'm not sure I would have felt that *any* man was "good enough" to be with my mom. Since I had directed all my hurt toward my mom, and because it felt like she had let me down by not staying married to my father, my heart became too hardened to allow myself to be close to her. Even though she wasn't going out on dates every weekend, I still convinced myself that she was choosing the men she dated over me and our family. I didn't like the lustful ways some of her dates looked at her, like she was an object to be consumed but not cherished. It felt like they had power over her. I also did not appreciate the way certain dates spoke disrespectfully to her. My heart began to distrust men. They seemed dangerous and unpredictable. When my mom put on her spicy, floral-scented Jean Nate perfume for a date, I would begin to panic, hating that my mom was leaving me. Even if she was just going for a quick bite to eat down the street with a friend, I would still frantically watch the clock and wait up for her to come home. I remember panicking on many occasions because she was late from working overtime or from a dinner date.

My mind would race and imagine the worst-case scenario. Because of my growing resentment toward my mom, nothing she could have said or done during this period would have felt right to me. One minute I convinced myself that I had the most inconsiderate mother in the whole world for causing me to worry. The next minute I was crying uncontrollably, imagining that she couldn't get home because her car had broken down after work and she was stranded on the side of the road, or that her date had taken advantage of her sexually.

Regarding the men my mom dated, I convinced myself that they were untrustworthy. I was vocal and would pick fights with her guy friends and dates. Some nights I would scream, "If you marry my mom, you'll be going against God's ways and living in sin!" I acted self-righteously and felt my actions were completely justified. I, arrogantly, felt I knew exactly what God's will was for our family.

My mom's personality was extremely friendly toward everyone she met. However, her friendliness toward men, especially men around her age, felt dangerous and aggravating to me. If we were at a grocery store, and I noticed the checker was flirting with her, I would step in and give him a rude comment and a glare. I did not like anyone she dated. The only way I knew how to make sure she was safe was to harden my heart toward men and treat them with contempt. I thought if I was mean to them, I would scare them away, and they would leave us alone. I missed the days when I had her full attention, and she didn't have to work long hours away from me. As a result of my anger and jealousy, I tried to "mother" my mom, rather than allow her to "mother" me. My controlling attitude became a wedge between us.

Then, in the eighth grade, I finally moved in with my dad, against my mom's pleadings to stay with her. Sadly, I had romanticized how wonderful it would be to live with him. I didn't admit it to my mom, but I quickly began to see why she had no longer felt safe being married to him. I lived with my dad from the eighth grade through the eleventh grade. During that time I experienced my dad as a complex and hypocritical man. Some days he was a generous and supportive father. On those days, he would model Christ's love. He taught me that we can cry out to God for help anywhere and anytime. For example, if we were driving to school and an ambulance would scream past us, he would immediately stop any previous conversation and lead us in praying for those involved in the accident. He was an extremely generous man. He worked long hours and always sacrificially provided for his children's needs. He also never missed any of my cross-country races or drama plays. He was always front and center, loudly cheering me on. Other days, though, he was full of discontent and rage. I became the target of his anger. His mood swings were unpredictable. I would never know what would set his anger off. I tried to be the "perfect" daughter by having the house clean, getting good grades, speaking to him respectfully, and always verbally appreciating the ways he provided for our family. But that didn't seem to be good enough. Some days, in the blink of an eye he would start yelling at me because I had bought the wrong type of soap at the store, or because I hadn't opened the box of raisin bran cereal exactly the way he had wanted me to open it. On occasion, he would yell and cuss at me so loud that the neighbors would yell from their own houses things like, "Shut the F*** up!" It was embarrassing leaving my house knowing that everyone on our block knew about our family drama.

Often, five minutes later my dad would be smiling, asking me how my geometry test went that day at school, acting like his verbal attack against me hadn't just happened. Other days he would seem depressed, unable to get out of bed till ten or eleven o'clock in the morning. Those days he acted like an ungrateful child, content to swim in pools of self-pity for the way his life had turned out. With my dad, I felt like I had to be the strong one emotionally. I became his surrogate spouse. I knew way too much about his mental and financial struggles, and I tried to make sure he was eating properly, taking care of himself, and feeling happy. I am saddened that my dad felt so alone and unloved during much of his life. Unfortunately, it took years for my dad to seek the help he needed to deal with his emotional pain. But, I am grateful that eventually my dad did seek support through resources like counseling, where he began to do much personal work and receive the healing that God had for him. I also believe that much emotional healing has come into his life as a result of the supportive love he has received from my stepmom.

Even though my parents were divorced, they intentionally lived only five minutes away from each other. They wanted us kids to be able to see them both, as often as we wanted. When I'd stay with my mom, she would repeatedly try to get me to open up to her. It was clear that she wanted to be there for me regarding any questions I had concerning things that might be on my mind. She also wanted to teach me about things involving being a feminine young woman—anything from personal hygiene, to insights regarding clothes, hair, and makeup. I vividly remember her suggesting I wear my bangs feathered back, but I insisted on wearing them tightly curled forward. Looking back at my school pictures, I so wished I had listened to her. She would also ask me about my friendships and if I had any crushes on any boys at school. When she'd talk, I'd put my hands over my ears and walk away yelling, "I don't care what YOU think!" At this point, my parents had been divorced for over four years. But because of my mom's consistent decision to not reconcile with my dad and to instead date other men, men that I did not approve of, I daily let her know that I did not respect her. I worked hard to make sure we were nothing alike. If she told me to do something, I would do everything in my power to make sure I did the opposite. I can only imagine how difficult I was to live with at this time. My mom was unfairly the sole recipient of all my anger. I am saddened for the ways I treated my mom with disrespect. Because I hardened my heart toward her during these formative years, I missed out on receiving all the mothering and nurturing she desired to shower me with. Thankfully, during my senior year of high school, we lived together again and our relationship began to heal. Then in the years that followed, we both grew in our faith relationships with God, and she and I began to connect more on spiritual matters of the heart. In my early thirties we had the gift of living together. We no longer had a strained relationship, and I could now show her that I respected her. She is a beautiful and godly woman and my heart was open to receive her care, wisdom, and nurturing spirit. Her unconditional love and support during this time also encouraged me to start my own business (a private counseling practice). Those years were full of much laughter, delicious meals (which were waiting for me after work), and fun adventures dancing and exploring the beauty of Seattle together.

Even if there had been guys asking me out on dates during my teen years, I don't think I would have had the time or emotional energy to date them because I was, of my own choice, too busy being the firstborn "responsible one" at home. I feared marriage, because I dreaded ending up unhappily married and unhappily divorced, just like my parents.

Our relationships with our parents deeply affected Stephen's and my views on God, dating, marriage, and sex. Although our parents were the major players in our development, our intention in sharing these delicate details about them is not to condemn them. Stephen and I have been molded at times by the world's ideals, our peers' opinions, Satan's lies, and our own personalities; and thankfully, also by our parents' love and God's truth found in the Bible. We share about the painful years in order for the reader to later see all that God has done to bring healing and restoration in our relationships with our parents.

When I moved in with my dad in the eighth grade, I started at a new school because he lived in a different district. That first week I had to give a speech on a controversial topic for my speech class. The title of the speech I chose was "The 10 Benefits of *Waiting* till Marriage to Have Sex." At that time, I was fairly naïve. I'm not even sure I knew how sex really worked. Nonetheless, I had just read, at my dad's prompting, Josh McDowell's book entitled *Why Wait?: What You Need to Know About the Teen Sexuality*

Crisis.[1] The book is full of personal stories of heartache from men and women of various ages who had engaged in premarital sex. I remember crying as I read stories of broken hearts and lives full of regret and shame. My goal in giving the speech was to save my fellow classmates, as well as myself, from similar pain. I also wanted to encourage everyone with the truth that God knows what's best for us. Looking back, I am amazed at the boldness Jesus gave me, not to mention the strong conviction and faith that was planted in me at the young age of thirteen.

A classmate, who became a close friend, later said, "After you gave that sex talk, nobody knew what the heck to do with you!" Giving this speech was not exactly the best way to make new friends and fit in.

As I read the *Why Wait* book, I learned that sexual intimacy is about more than just a physical connection; a spiritual union happens as well. I saw that sex is a good and beautiful gift from God. This gift of sex is protected, blessed, and designed to be opened within the covenant of marriage. Sadly, I don't remember this positive view of sex being reiterated by the adults in my life. I didn't know if married couples I knew were having sex, let alone viewing it as a gift from the Lord. During my early teen years my mom tried to talk to me about sex a couple of times, but I shut her down immediately. Overall, sex was a subject that was ignored, which made it seem forbidden and shameful.

When sexuality was addressed at my church youth group, it was for the purpose of telling me all the things I should not be doing with boys. It felt like all the responsibility was on the woman to make sure sex didn't happen. I was left feeling that sex was bad, dirty, and a burden.

In high school, there was only one Christian guy I knew that I would have considered dating, and he was a close friend of mine. I was thrilled when he asked me to prom. He had a lively personality, and we laughed a lot when we were together. I designed my own prom dress. The dress, made of emerald green satin, had puffy, slightly off-the-shoulder sleeves and arms decked out in sheer black lace. At the time it felt oh so fashionable. Nothing romantic ever happened between us.

I had a full schedule in high school. I ran cross-country, did drama, studied for hours on end, and worked at a local frozen yogurt shop. I was usually too busy to care that guys weren't asking me to see the latest movies with them on the weekends. But, some nights I felt tired of feeling unnoticed. I remember crying to my dad one evening when I was about fourteen about how no guy would ever like me and ask me out. He lovingly said, "Honey, you just tell everyone that you have a really mean dad that won't let you date until you're nineteen." Living with my dad was not easy. I felt like I never knew if he was going to explode with anger or not, but in that brief moment, I experienced the loving and wise man God had created. I was grateful that his comments gave us both a chance to laugh together.

When I was in college I made amazing friendships. For the first time in my life I had a group of Christian girlfriends. My closest friends at Westmont College hadn't dated much, if at all, either. We were kindred sisters. Aside from the occasional crushes we would have on guys and the subsequent longing for dates, we were mostly quite content hanging out with each other on Friday nights.

My first "almost" boyfriend came after college, when I was twenty-two. He'd bring me huge containers of cookies 'n' cream ice cream from the shop he worked at. I'd accompany him on weekends to the weddings and parties he would deejay. At the end of our hang-out times, he'd always awkwardly give me an enthusiastic high five. Eventually, I sensed he wanted to take our relationship to the next level. I wanted to have the desire to be his girlfriend. He was such a great guy, but in the end I knew that remaining "just friends" was all I wanted. After hanging out with him for almost a year, I introduced him to a friend of mine. They've been happily married for over a decade now.

My first "official" boyfriend, "official" in that we called each other "boyfriend" and "girlfriend," came when I was twenty-four. My first kiss also came while dating this boyfriend. Waiting this long to have my first kiss felt like *forever*. An explosion of fireworks did not go off during my first kiss. I felt clumsy, and the whole thing was wet and awkward. But, I was relieved that I could now honestly join in the frequent conversations with girlfriends about kissing. I'm embarrassed to admit that on occasion I lied and said my first kiss happened earlier than it actually did.

With this first dating relationship, and with many that followed, my mom encouraged me to stay true to myself and my strong belief that sex is a beautiful gift from God, worth waiting for. Looking back though, I wish my parents and other important adults in my life had shared with me, at a younger age, compelling reasons for staying sexually pure. But I realize that my parents were human, doing the best they could. Neither of them had a loving and faithful marriage modeled for them. They also came from divorced homes. And, sadly, they both endured sexual trauma and abuse growing up.

I am thankful that the generational sin of divorce stops with Stephen and me. I pray that Stephen and I have open and honest communication about sexuality with our children, from a young age. I want to share with them that sex is a glorious gift and that we're so glad we waited to enjoy this gift with each other as husband and wife. Also, I hope that when we fail our children, or each other, we will be quick to ask for forgiveness.

Forgiveness has been crucial in my life. It is what brought me close to my parents after many painful years of feeling distant from them. I am thankful that over the years, both of my parents humbled themselves and asked me to forgive them for the ways they had hurt and failed me as parents. In 2003, to my surprise, God showed me that I had not completely accepted my parents' apologies. I was still harboring resentments toward them both. At that time, I was headed to Washington State to start graduate school, where I would be getting a master's degree in counseling. On my long drive from Long Beach to Seattle, I listened to a sermon series on forgiveness that a good friend had just loaned to me. It was a convicting car ride. The Lord gave me a vivid glimpse of myself as an older woman. He showed me that if I did not release my hurts and resentments to Him, I would become a bitter, hunched-over woman with a dark and cloudy heart, closed off to people. The sermon series talked about forgiveness being a one-time event as well as an ongoing process. I distinctly remember somehow getting to the place where I cried out to God, "Lord, I need you. I'm tired of having anger and bitterness toward my parents. I want to move on! In your strength, I forgive my mom and my dad for the ways they have disappointed and hurt me over the years." (I named the different ways I felt I had been wronged). It was a simple prayer. God empowered me to pray it. From that day forward, a huge shift took place, and I began to share more of my true heart with my parents. I felt more open to letting them parent me, and letting them offer me their wisdom and advice.

Shortly after I moved to Seattle, I got asked out on a date by a fellow counseling student. We went on to have the best date I'd ever had, up until that point. I immediately called my mom to tell her all about it. It was fun to rave about what an enjoyable and lighthearted time we had. I shared how my date and I played like five-year-old kids at a local playground, visited a pawn shop (because I had never been to one before), and found cozy chairs at an antique shop, where my date read me an excerpt from one of my favorite books, *Les Misérables*. This was the first time I can recall ever really inviting my mom into my dating life. It felt vulnerable, but also wonderful, sharing this part of my life with her. Before Christ freed me from my weight of bitterness, I never would have shared this experience with her.

Throughout much of my adult life I have wondered, "Why *am* I waiting to have sex, and why am I believing that God has my best interest in mind?" I often felt like I was the only one in the whole world *still* single and still waiting. Periodically asking myself, "Why *am* I waiting?" is a wonderful question because it's an opportunity for me to be completely real, regroup, and have my vision strengthened. For me, the conviction to wait had been strong at times, and other times it had waned. Unfortunately, most often my conviction was *wait till marriage to have sex*, and not *live a life of purity*. My goal of staying a virgin did not mean I always stayed sexually pure. There are many sexual acts that one can do while still remaining "technically" a virgin. Sadly, for many years my mind-set was *have as much fun as possible; just make sure you don't go all the way*. I wish I had thought more about what it means to stay mentally and physically pure.

Some days it didn't feel like God cared about my love life. It seemed like everyone but me was happily dating or happily married. On those days, Christ seemed far away from the sexual temptations I was facing. I'm grateful that even when I was angry at God for not making it all easier, or even when I lived out of a self-centered or self-righteous place regarding my sexuality, God never gave up on me.

I've known, perhaps ever since giving that speech on the benefits of waiting for sex when I was thirteen, that part of my purpose and calling on this earth involves waiting. Even now, as I write this book with my husband about waiting with God for His best, I see that my sexuality and my destiny have always been connected. This call to wait with God has not always seemed significant enough to share. Now I see how rich and rewarding my life has been because of the times I waited with God, instead of forcing things to happen on my own timetable. If I had tried to plan and plot my life in my own wisdom, I know that my life would have been significantly less fulfilling. I would have played it safe and missed out on the grand adventures that led me to work all over the world with troubled teenagers, university students, homeless men and women, and people from all walks of life who felt hopeless and lost.

For me, it became bigger than just waiting to have sex, or waiting for Him to bring me my future husband. Christ's invitation was to come to Him and talk with Him about every matter in my life, big or small. Being married to Stephen has been well worth the wait indeed!

For Reflection:

1. How would you describe your growing-up years? What did you find your security in?
2. What have been your experiences of waiting? Are you in a season of waiting? What do you want to say to Jesus about this? Take time to be with the Creator to see if He has anything He wants to say to you as you wait.
3. Are you waiting until marriage to have sex? If so, why? If you're not sure why you're waiting, take time to ask the Lord for His wisdom and insights. If you haven't waited and wish you had, you can recommit yourself at this time. (It's never too late!)

CHAPTER 2

Something is missing

Stephen Reflects:

I was a late bloomer. I began puberty somewhere between my seventeenth and eighteenth birthdays, thus experiencing quite a bit of insecurity about my body. I dreaded showering and changing in the locker room, and I worked hard to stay hidden from my peers. I felt like I was the only one who had the body of a young boy. It was quite embarrassing that sixth-grade girls had crushes on me when I was a junior in high school. Staying sexually pure wasn't a huge challenge at this point in my life because my body had not matured yet and I felt insecure to pursue women.

My dad left when I was eleven months old. I now know that he left at twenty-three when he realized that he didn't want to be tied down to a wife and family. However, growing up, I felt like my dad left because there was something wrong with *me*. I thought maybe I wasn't good enough. This wasn't something I verbally expressed, but it was something I believed in my heart. These feelings continued for years, and in my twenties I verbalized it all in a conversation with my pastor. "I feel so condemned. I know God's Word says He loves me, but why do I feel such a deep sense of shame?"

Many children of divorce feel this way. I know this because of my own experience, from books I have read, and from my work as a psychotherapist. I don't remember my mom saying much about my dad and why he left. And I don't remember asking much about him, nor do I remember my older brother asking these questions. I mainly felt my mom's grief regarding my dad's absence. Therefore, I chose to not broach the subject with her for fear of causing her further heartache.

My mom dated some after the divorce. Even though many of the guys were okay, I mostly remember ignoring them. I didn't want any guy taking her attention away from me. When her dates would introduce themselves and reach out to shake our hands, my brother and I would, with arms crossed, glare at them in disgust and walk away. Eventually my mom became a Christian, and as she grew in her relationship with God, she came to the conclusion that God was inviting her to look to *Him* to be her husband, rather than a man. The fact that my mom stopped dating came as a relief because it meant that her commitment and devotion were to my brother and me.

My dad returned when I was six years old to be near us and to be a father to me and my brother. My first memory of him is of me riding on a Big Wheel in our driveway, and I saw a car drive up and a man with a beard get out. At that moment, our front door burst open and my older brother, David, ran across our front lawn and jumped into this man's arms. I saw all of this, and I walked over, looked up at this man, and with flatness in my voice asked, "Are you my dad?"

Even though my dad was now back in our life on the weekends, I felt like he was a stranger to me. Soon after he came back, I decided I did not want to go see him that regularly. It was painful to leave my mother and go to my dad's, and then it was painful to leave my dad and go back to my mom; it felt emotionally draining. However, I would go once in awhile when my brother would plead with me to go with him.

Added to all of this was my father's decision to remarry when I was about seven. He married my stepmom, who had two daughters from a previous marriage. I liked my stepmom and stepsisters; however, the dream of my dad and mom ever getting back together died. This was my dad's choice, not mine, and I resisted being a part of two families. It almost felt like I was betraying my mom when I spent time with my dad and his new family. I think I picked up on my mom's coldness toward my dad and I followed suit. I never once saw my mom talk with my dad or stepmom. When my dad would come and get us for the weekend, he would knock on the door and my brother and I would meet him at the door. You could literally feel the tension in the air between my parents. At soccer games and school events it was painfully awkward. I felt I had to be the one to accommodate my mom and make sure she didn't have to interact with my dad and experience further pain and grief. I sensed my mother's anguish. She tried to keep her sorrows from us by crying in her bedroom. But it was a small house, and I heard her tears. And since I was more bonded with her, and had consistently felt her love, I was hesitant to form a close relationship with my father. I chose to remain distant, even though he continued to pursue a relationship with me.

It wasn't until I was about twelve that I decided to go see my dad more regularly. Looking back, it was most likely a result of a developmental need that many boys have at this age to be around their dads. Over the years, I continued to struggle with how close to allow my dad and my stepfamily to get to my heart. As a kid and teenager, I didn't know how to deal with all these emotions. I chose to bury them and stayed busy playing soccer and basketball, studying, hanging out with my guy friends, and being the all-around "good" Christian kid. It wasn't until college that I began to deal more honestly with my hurts and disappointments.

Sadly, my mom and brother have had a tense and strained relationship for as long as I can remember. Because my mom didn't have a husband, I felt like I had to be the one to jump in and protect her when she and my brother argued.

Since I felt like I had to be the one to defend my mom, a certain type of chasm formed between my brother and me. I didn't think my mom handled everything perfectly, but I wanted her to know I was in her corner and I wanted peace in the home. My brother has said that while I was protecting my mom, he felt like he had to protect me, mom, and dad. I am saddened by the ways that he and I both felt like we had to step in and protect each other and our parents, a role that kids should not be burdened with. I regret not developing a closer and healthier relationship with my brother when we were younger. Thankfully, God has freed me today to be my mom's son and not her spouse, or her defender. And, I am now free to be my brother's brother and friend.

Also, not having my dad around was difficult because I had to learn how to be a man on my own. He was not around to teach me how to throw a baseball, fix the kitchen sink if it broke, or treat a woman with love and tenderness. I have a memory from when I was around twelve of my dad giving my brother and me "the sex talk." For most people, it is an awkward conversation to have, but because of the emotional distance between my dad and me, it felt even more uncomfortable. I am grateful that at least he tried. During the years when I didn't feel bonded to my dad, God provided other male role models.

In essence, I missed out on my father teaching me how to be a man. Thus, I developed some significant self-esteem issues. Outwardly, I appeared to be more confident than I was because I did fairly well academically and athletically. However, there was an internal battle going on, and I did not feel confident. As a result, I did not develop a healthy sense of self.

Instead of "finding my own voice," I was too busy trying to "people please." I was afraid to let anyone down. Years later, with the help of a caring psychotherapist, I realized that I wanted other people's approval in order to overcome the disapproval I felt toward myself. The problem was that this was never enough. It could never fill that hole. Even though I had a lot of amazing friends, who genuinely cared about me, I still felt empty and alone much of the time. I had a fear of rejection that kept me from taking risks in every area of my life, including my interactions with women.

Also, I was really afraid of getting a divorce like my parents. I knew firsthand how devastating it was on the kids. There were many moments where I felt like my heart was torn in two. Thus, I did not want to risk inflicting this kind of emotional pain on my children.

In high school, I did have one "girlfriend," and when I broke up with her, she was deeply hurt and I was left feeling like a jerk. As a result of this dating experience and observing my mom, I resolved to never put a woman through such pain again. Therefore, I kept women at an arm's length, not allowing them to get too close. I played it safe and protected my heart, even though some would say I was being a noble guy respecting and protecting girls' hearts. I was afraid to truly love anyone, because I didn't want my heart to ever be broken again, as it was when my dad left. C. S. Lewis's words resonated with me: "To love at all is to be vulnerable. Love anything, and your heart will certainly be wrung and possibly broken. If you want to make sure of keeping it intact, you must give your heart to no one."[2]

I usually ended things with girls after one or two dates, and I made sure that I kept things in the "friend zone" by not kissing these girls I took out. I subconsciously thought that if I kissed a girl, I would be breaking God's rules and not honoring women, because the Bible says that we are to treat younger women as sisters with absolute purity (1 Timothy 5:2). I'm grateful for God's guidance in this area of honoring women. I respected God and believed that His way was the best way to a fulfilled life. But, the part that grieves me is the belief that if I did the slightest thing wrong He would abandon me.

Then, in college, as I started getting more serious with a girlfriend, I felt like there wasn't room in my life for both her and God. This is the point in my life where if I didn't spend at least an hour with God in the morning, I felt like God wasn't with me that day. I felt that God wouldn't want me to have anything good in my life, including this girlfriend. Subconsciously, I believed that if *I* desired something, such as a dating relationship, then it must not be from God. My desires seemed less than God's ultimate good for me. It wasn't until years later that I began to see the importance of listening to my heart and paying attention to the passions and desires that God has planted there. God can lead me through my desire.

While I was wrestling with God as to what to do about this dating relationship, she broke up with me. I now see clearly that I believed lies about who God was and His true heart of love toward me. God is a good God who desires for me to have a loving relationship with Him *and* close connections with others. I was created for intimacy.

As a follower of Christ, I was taught that the best place for great sex was between two married people. I took that seriously, mostly for the wrong reason—I was afraid God would not love me if I messed up His rules. Prior to early adulthood, I viewed God as a harsh taskmaster whom I had to perfectly please so that He wouldn't withhold His love and abandon me, like my father had. It is interesting how our view of God often resembles how we view our own fathers. The sacred Scriptures read, "When I was a child, my speech, feelings, and thinking were all those of a child; now that I am an adult, I have no more use for childish ways" (1 Corinthians 13:11). It was not until my midtwenties, through the help of my psychotherapist and other friends and mentors, that I began to put childish thinking and the belief systems of my childhood behind me and experience God in a more accurate light. No longer did I just intellectually know truth about God's character, but now I felt it on a heart level. God was my loving Father who cared about me and would never leave me.

Throughout my college years and most of my early twenties, I struggled with significant depression. I believe that my depression was related to the effects of my parents' divorce and the thoughts and belief systems I chose to embrace. At one point, I was so depressed that I almost dropped out of Wheaton College, near Chicago, where I was attending. I did make it to graduation, but shortly after, I was basically a hermit living at my mom's house. My typical Friday night included me ordering take-out stromboli from the local pizza joint, playing a competitive Scrabble game with my mom at home, and retiring to bed around nine thirty. Let's just say that this lifestyle did not have girls knocking at my door!

After a while, I did move out of my mom's house. Eventually, I started dating an intriguing woman. She was attractive and had many qualities I admired. She was a teacher in an inner city and desired to share God's love with the poor. This relationship didn't last too long, as she broke up with me. At the time, I was devastated and was left wondering why she had ended it, as she didn't give me any reasons. Looking back, it probably was because I was not living connected to my heart and with passion. I was still discovering who I was and what I felt God had called me to do vocationally.

This breakup felt like a rejection. Yet again, I was left asking, "Why was I left?" This ending was pivotal to me receiving more healing and freedom. It created in me a deeper desire for relationship. It was similar to a person who has a physical wound that they haven't cared for. It typically will fester, and most likely an infection will grow with further devastating results. A doctor or nurse will need to cut open the wound, clean out the infection, and then close up the wound. This is an incredibly painful process, yet necessary for healing. I believe God used this relationship to "cut me open" so that I could further heal emotionally.

It was also during this time that I explored and wrestled with God's vocational calling on my life. I took on all sorts of jobs. Blue-collar, white-collar, nonprofit, and teaching—I tried the gamut. At twenty-nine, I left a high school teaching position to ride my bike across the U.S. with friends. It was just what my soul needed—adventure, beauty, community, a physical challenge, and a worthy mission. The goal was to raise money and advertize for a newly licensed Christian college in my home state of New Jersey.

I came back from this trip reenergized and excited about working with my father on a more focused search for my calling. As I had begun to heal, my relationship with my father was also beginning to mend. And I was now more willing to open my heart up to him. I am thankful that he consistently pursued me for those many years. Finally, what I had longed for from my father all my life (guidance) was being fulfilled at age twenty-nine. Having spent most of his business career in the human resource development field, he led me through a series of exercises to help me narrow down my dream job. This experience was bigger than just about discovering my dream job; it was about connecting with my dad and receiving significant healing. A few months later, I decided to pursue the counseling profession.

It was a prayerful decision, as well as an act of faith, to move from New Jersey to Colorado to attend graduate school, where I pursued a master's in counseling at Denver Seminary. It was a fantastic move for me, and the expansiveness and beauty of the Rocky Mountains did wonders for my soul. Colorado is a land of adventure and risk. My first year there I bought a Colorado mountain pass, and I enjoyed midweek jaunts to some of the major resorts, such as Vail and Breckenridge, and spent many days carving up mountains with my snowboard. I enjoyed these days of communing with God in His beautiful and wild creation. I also loved hiking fourteen-thousand-foot peaks, camping, and fishing in the rugged wilderness.

My heart became freer. Since I was more confident with who I was, I became more open to dating. I soon found myself in a serious relationship with a young woman whom I thought might be "the one."

We looked good "on paper," as we both enjoyed the outdoors, cycling, soccer, and other sports. Our relationship had mostly been long distance, and I eventually moved to her hometown. The day before moving, at a party, I overheard a close friend saying, "Yeah, Stephen's moving out to the

Western Slope. He's in love." I just remember thinking, "Yeah, I am moving, but I'm not quite sure I'm in love."

My girlfriend and I had a difficult time relating to each other and connecting on a "heart" level. One time when I was praying with her, she said, "No, let's *really* pray" (as if I wasn't being authentic enough). This left me feeling shut down and judged. I doubt she was aware that I felt this way. On a different occasion I remember telling her, "As a counselor, I spend much of my day drawing people out, asking questions, and getting to hear the deepest desires of my clients' hearts. Because I'm more of an introvert, it would help me open up more if you asked *me* more questions. I do want to be known on a deeper level." She sounded open to my request, but there was never any follow-up.

When I would visit her, hungry after a long day at work, I had to bring fast food over, because the hospitality was quite lacking. It is not that I expected her to have a meal ready for me every night, but occasionally saving me some leftovers from her meal would have helped me feel valued and appreciated. Toward the end of our relationship, I had the exciting opportunity to speak at a Christian ministry that I believed was doing amazing things to share God's love. My girlfriend did not believe in the mission of this ministry, and I realized that she had, in my opinion, some legalistic views about God's heart, specifically toward people struggling with sexual sins. At the time I remembered the wise words of a mentor: "Can you see yourself serving God together?" In this relationship my answer was no. I did not feel supported by her as I stepped into ministry opportunities that I believed Christ was calling me to be a part of. After two years of dating, I realized that, while there was much I admired about this woman, she ultimately was not the person I wanted to spend the rest of my life with, and I ended the relationship.

After the breakup I found myself a lonely bachelor in limbo land for about four years. I didn't want to continue to pursue her, but it was hard for me to see myself pursuing someone else. During my thirty-seventh year I wrote the following thoughts on loneliness:

Thoughts on Loneliness
An ache . . .

Our greatest fear and our greatest need are the same thing: to be known.

The ache of loneliness leads a person to many places to soothe the ache. Could it be that most of our addictions are because of loneliness?

I can understand why young people might cut themselves; the physical pain relieves the emotional pain we feel.

"It is not good for man to be alone"—God. Did Christ feel the ache of loneliness? "My God, my God, why have you forsaken me?"

*God longs to fill this ache in us. He longs to
be with us, to have a close relationship with us.
His name shall be called "Emanuel, God with
us." This is Christmas—God with us.*

*What about the single person? How does he/she cope
with this loneliness? What about the married person?
Does he/she ever experience loneliness? I would
suppose sometimes, perhaps some more than others,
depending upon the quality of the marriage.*

*I write this because I feel lonely often. Like no one really
wants to know me. Or is it because I close them off
before they get too close? It is definitely safer that way.
Who will set me free from this? As a single man, almost
37, it does not feel right to be single. I am feeling like I
should have a bride; something is missing, like a part
of me, a rib perhaps, something very deep and soulful.
Sure, I have had some opportunities for a bride, but they
have come to an end; and in the end, I never really felt
known or perhaps I never allowed that to happen.*

I imagine many have felt something similar. After God created everything, He said it was good, except for one thing: "It is not good for man to be alone!" The first man (Adam) enjoyed intimate fellowship with God. He walked with Him in the Garden of Eden, yet this was not enough to fill the ache in Adam. To say that almost sounds blasphemous—God not being enough! But, that is how the sacred Scriptures read. Perhaps it is because man was created in the image of God. Core to the image of God is community—Father, Son, and Holy Spirit. Man was made in God's image; thus he was made with a need for community. Marriage, as God initiated it and at its best, is the most intimate of relationships and is the richest expression of community.

On May 9, 2009, a year before meeting Rebecca, my dad wrote me the following words: "You need to be honest with yourself and take the risk to once and for all discover if indeed (your ex-girlfriend) is right for you. You tend to be risk adverse in your relationships, and you need to make it a priority if you want to have someone share in your life. That means putting effort and time into it. Whatever you decide I will always love you unconditionally. I just want you to be happy and feel fulfilled. You are a special person, Stephen—trust that and push yourself. Time to get moving!"

I was thankful that my dad courageously took the time to write me a challenging letter like this. It was difficult, but also motivating, for me to hear my dad name my struggle with decision making. I got together with my ex-girlfriend for a date and realized once and for all that she was not the woman God had for me.

During this season I was also receiving personal counseling. God used these sessions to bring healing, and He broke lingering emotional ties to her. Six months later

God exposed this lie: *I will never marry because it's too painful and the risk is too great.* Exposing and breaking this lie was incredibly significant. At the close of this counseling session, my counselor prayed and blessed my future marriage. I left feeling new freedom.

I didn't stay a wounded and lost boy. Instead I emerged, thanks to God's healing work in my life, as a strong and confident man of God, with a heart open to receiving my heavenly Father's and my earthly father's love and guidance.

For Reflection:

1. What did your parents and/or other significant adults in your life communicate to you about dating, marriage, and sex?
2. Share about your spiritual journey. What brings you joy and fulfillment? (We wish there was a way to sit down with each of you over a cup of coffee to hear about your experiences of the Divine.)
3. Take time to ask God how He feels about you.
4. If you have kids, bring to God any regrets you have as a parent. Ask Him to lead you in asking for, and receiving, forgiveness. Take time to extend grace and forgiveness toward yourself.

CHAPTER 3

He'll be worth the wait

Rebecca Reflects:

If you're anything like me, then a thousand times you've asked questions like, "Where is he? When will my dream be realized? When will my prayers finally be answered?"

Throughout my life, I have experienced much emotional relief by writing my thoughts and feelings down in a journal. It's a way for me to surrender even the confusing and hard parts of my life to Jesus' care. Here are some of God's promises that have encouraged me over the years regarding my future husband and marriage. I share them in the hope that you will be encouraged by my story, and also challenged to begin to record and savor the truths and promises you've been given along your journey.

In November 1999, I had a vision during an evening church service where I was on staff. I saw myself with my future husband. We were standing up front, holding hands, praying for others who were in need of God's healing. In this vision, I saw that we would partner together to care for hurting people.

In July 2001, I was living at a YWAM (Youth with a Mission) base in the Tenderloin district of San Francisco. My job was to lead church youth groups on daily outreaches in the city. We had many opportunities for ministry, such as sharing sack lunches with homeless people. One day, a group of junior high students and I were visiting with a man who had been living as a woman. He had been faithfully coming to YWAM's Sunday morning church services. His heart was open to God. After the students and I shared with him Christ's love and how God had brought positive change and peace to our lives, he too wanted to have a personal relationship with Jesus.

It was a powerful time of visiting and praying. Later, he told me that God wanted me to know that I would, indeed, be married. He also said that the marriage would be very good, but that I would be waiting for marriage for some time. While his words were bittersweet, and the prophetic nature of them was definitely unexpected, they did resonate with my spirit.

Another powerful interaction occurred in December 2002. While working in Brooklyn, New York, with an organization that reached out to children in the community, I met a woman who had written a book about marriage. After reading her book, I was challenged by the powerful impact a praying wife can have on her husband and her family's life. This author seemed like a woman who walked closely with God. I asked if she would be willing to meet with me to pray for my future husband and marriage. We met, and I appreciated her heartfelt and bold prayers for me, someone she had just met. I was struck by how well she knew her authority and identity as God's daughter. She was the first person who had ever confidently, in Jesus' power, prayed against the attacks of evil made against me. A few days later, she gave me a letter she had written full of more truths that God had given her regarding my future spouse. Here is a small portion from the fifteen-page letter she presented to me.

> *Nothing has been a waste of time. The devil's plans to destroy you and hold you back were thwarted. Now you are going forward. I see you calm, rested, and teaching others to live the same way. I see you on a stage, Rebecca, speaking to a large group of people. The gift of exhortation is in full swing. I see you pouring pure love and compassion on the people. But it is God's love that you are pouring into them, and not yours, and God's love does not get depleted!*
>
> *You will have a marriage full of joy, delight, and fun. Yet, your marriage will serve a HIGH PURPOSE also. You are to support your husband. Keep looking to God to meet all your needs. Because you continuously go to the Lord for **everything** and are continuously fed by Him, you will be a TREASURE to your husband.*

> *You and your husband's ministry will be a BIG ministry, influencing many, many, people.*

I still have her letter. It has water stains on it now, ink is smeared, and the pages are wrinkled. Each time I read this letter over the years I received fresh encouragement from God, inspiration to keep on waiting for His loving timing and plan for my future marriage.

In April 2005, as I was listening to "Echo Park" by one of my favorite musicians, Joseph Arthur, in my heart I dedicated this song to my future husband. Here is part of the chorus: "Freedom and freedom our love won't fade away . . . the light of love pouring down." After I listened to the song, I heard Christ speak to me: "Keep hoping in Me, Rebecca." I love that this Joseph Arthur song was the first song our guests heard as they visited our wedding website six years later.

In August 2005, I had a glimpse of God that was definitely "outside the box." Here's what I wrote in my journal:

> *God, you sit and squirm on the edge*
> *of your chair,*
> *giddy as a young school girl*
>
> *holding a secret in the palm*
> *of your sweaty hand.*

Can you wait a moment longer,
or will you burst with joy?

Christ is my Lord and Savior, but God's character doesn't end there. God is many wonderful things. Jesus is playful, full of passion, and has a heart to bless us. Wow! As I reflect on this poem, I see that I'm not the only one who has been waiting. Christ has been waiting too. He waited many years before introducing me to the wonderful man I would marry.

> *October 2006: "Though it linger, wait for it; it will certainly come and will not delay" (Habakkuk 2:3). The Lord tells Habakkuk and Judah (and me) that fulfillment of the prophecy may "linger," but we can expect it. My husband may linger, but deep in my heart I know that he does exist, and he will come.*

> *January 2008: During a spiritual director's retreat near Seattle, I had a vision. I was standing near a cliff, looking expectantly out at the vast expanse of unpredictable waters. I wrote:*
>
> *Two sailboats*
> *separate journeys*
> *turning toward each other*
> *Coming home*

> *My heart's desire is to move past all other men and distractions and into the arms of my husband. Now, I see more clearly why my future husband and I have not yet met. We couldn't have because we were in different parts of the sea, on different adventures. I look forward to sharing our travels and adventures with each other. I pray that our paths would cross soon.*

In the same month, my mom had a dream that we were toasting with champagne to my future marriage engagement.

A month later, my heart was encouraged by the following quote by author Alice Walker: "I have learned not to worry about love, but to honor its coming with all my heart."

In April 2008, I wrote the following poem:

> *Twirling me in my sassy black dress,*
> *laughing*
> *rejoicing to be in his arms,*
> *alive to God's goodness.*

> *July 2008: There has been a lot about being single that I have liked. I enjoyed going to happy hour, concerts, and out dancing at the Century Ballroom with friends, and sleeping in whenever I wanted to. It was wonderful being independent and free, and only feeling*

responsible for myself. But, as I'm about to turn thirty-three, I now join my other single girlfriends in saying, "Being single and free is overrated. I WANT to be married!"

At this time I began spending more and more lonely nights with nothing but a romantic comedy and a microwavable macaroni cheese dinner from Trader Joe's to keep me company. As I lived vicariously through Meg Ryan's or Sandra Bullock's character I wondered when I would start living my own love story. Often I would go to bed feeling frustrated and angry at God for not saving me from yet another boring Saturday night. Even if it was a Saturday when I'd been out Salsa dancing with friends, I often still came home feeling unsatisfied with my relationship status. When I was out with girlfriends, we would usually meet guys, but I wasn't meeting quality guys that I was excited about dating.

Stephen Reflects:

My typical Saturday evening included activities like going for a long bike ride up the Colorado National Monument, ballroom dancing, or hanging out with friends for a BBQ. My quieter evenings were spent at home reading epic adventures like J. R. R. Tolkien's *Lord of the Rings*. Even though I enjoyed my single life and had good friends, I often found myself wrestling with loneliness.

Rebecca Reflects:

I'm grateful that I didn't always choose to stay stuck in a place of self-pity. Sometimes I would cry out to the Lord and tell Him all about my disappointments regarding feeling unloved and unchosen. It was during these hopeless nights that God would remind me that He loved spending time with me and that I could trust my love life into His capable and loving hands.

May 2009 ushered in a season where it was on my heart to do more than just pray for my future husband. I felt inspired to create a tangible gift that I could one day give to him. I decided to get together a group of my closest Seattle girlfriends. That night we shared a delicious meal. Then we waited in sacred silence to be led how to pray for my future husband. Out of our prayer time, each of my girlfriends made a collage card for my future husband and me. On the card, they each wrote out a prayer for our marriage. Here are some of their prayers:

> *Envisioning Rebecca and her husband united as King and Queen, holding much responsibility as they serve many people (their Kingdom), bringing God's presence and healing light to dark and wounded places.*
>
> *May you always cherish your God and yourselves, so you will be able to cherish one another. You will create beauty, joy and laughter in your moments together. You will be blessed*

with much and content with one another. I pray great blessings upon you both and your beautiful, healthy, pure, and holy love.

May God richly bless your sexual relationship. I pray for an abundance of gentleness, forgiveness, passion, grace, love, pleasure, hope, acceptance, honesty, growth, and adventure. May your relationship be a place where God's beauty and presence are so deeply felt that you are led to worship.

In February 2010, I wrote this in my journal:

During the sermon at church today God was speaking directly to me. I heard, "Marriage will come at just the right time." My only hope is in the Lord and in His faithfulness.

In light of this, I love how the hymn "Great Is Thy Faithfulness" was beautifully sung by a dear friend at our wedding ceremony.

I am grateful for all the ways, big and small, God spoke to me about my future marriage. Even when I wasn't always listening, He was faithfully speaking. I have learned a lot from the Biblical character Rebecca. My favorite promise was God showing me that He would be my matchmaker, like He was with Rebecca and Isaac in the Bible. It's amazing to me just how personally involved God desires to be in our romantic lives. He really does know us by name.

Stephen Reflects:

Unlike Rebecca, I did not have specific promises from God that I clung to regarding my future marriage. It wasn't until I was twenty-eight that I even thought about wanting to get married. I don't ever remember asking God questions regarding my love life. I'm not sure I even knew how to start a conversation like that. The reflection questions from our book would have aided me in discovering the truest and deepest desire of my heart. All that I was blaringly aware of was my fear of ending up divorced, like my parents. This prevented me from getting too close to women. During graduate school, when I was thirty, after much counseling and healing, I realized that I did want to be married. Also, it wasn't until 2002 that I first started believing that I can actually hear God's voice. This was the year when I was deciding whether to move to Colorado for graduate school.

As I stepped out in faith and went to grad school, I began to attend spiritual retreats hosted by author John Eldredge. As a result of these retreats, I started to hear God speak to me directly. It seems like a simple thing now, but I was never taught that there are different voices that we need to discern: God's, the world's, the evil one's, and my own. I began to learn that the condemning and negative messages I was hearing were not from God. One of the first things Christ told me was "Stephen, I love you, and I am proud of you."

For Reflection:

1. Have you received promises and encouragement regarding what your heart most longs for? If so, take time remembering and reflecting on them. If not, ask God to speak to you.
2. Has Jesus ever spoken to you specifically about your future spouse and marriage? If so, what are the themes of what you have heard so far? If not, take time to ask Christ if He has anything specific for you at this time.
3. Read the Scripture below and ask the Lord Jesus to speak to you.

All around us we observe a pregnant creation. The difficult times of pain throughout the world are simply birth pangs. But it's not only around us; it's within us. The Spirit of God is arousing us within. We're also feeling the birth pangs. These sterile and barren bodies of ours are yearning for full deliverance. That is why waiting does not diminish us, any more than waiting diminishes a pregnant mother. We are enlarged in the waiting. We, of course, don't see what is enlarging us. But the longer we wait, the larger we become, and the more joyful our expectancy.(Romans 8:23—25, The Message)

CHAPTER 4

I will be dating my future husband by my 35th birthday

Rebecca Reflects:

My final six months of being single were a season of crucial growth and refinement. During this time, my roommate introduced me to Katherine Woodward Thomas's book *Calling in "The One": 7 Weeks to Attract the Love of Your Life*, which was another tool God used to open my heart to marriage. As I began to complete the journaling exercises in the book, I realized that in the past, I was left feeling unfulfilled in most of my dating relationships. I did not want this pattern to continue, and I began to visualize what I most hoped for in my marriage. My new mantra became *"My life is full of intimacy and soul-felt connection."* Katherine Woodward Thomas's book challenged me to give up my attachment to what I thought my future husband should look and act like. When I would daydream, a certain "type" of guy would often come to my mind. He would always be perfectly patient, loving, and emotionally stable. He would be tall, but not too tall, and have deep, clear, blue eyes and dark, disheveled hair that was the perfect combination between short and long. He would play the guitar effortlessly, surf like Kelly Slater (without feeling the need to compete professionally), and have a chiseled six-pack (that didn't require hours spent away from me at the gym). He'd surprise me with exciting plans on Friday nights. His personality would be as relaxed and easygoing as a Jack Johnson song. Our communication and relationship would flow easily, and our days would be conflict free and full of bliss. I began to realize that in order to move forward, I would need to release control over how I thought my love story should unfold. I would need to let go of this superficial fantasy of my ideal mate in order to receive the real-life man that God had for me.

Katherine Woodward Thomas's book also encouraged me to reflect on the types of men who were showing up in my life. The men I had dated were usually directionless and boring. My dating pattern was to date weak and passive men. I dated men who did not challenge me or pursue the deepest places of my heart. I think it's important for me to share all this because it will help you see just what a gift Stephen's passionate, faithful, and focused presence is in my life today!

With my dad, and with my boyfriends, I worked hard to be perfect. I felt I had to look "put together" and be consistently happy in order to keep everyone else feeling happy and emotionally stable. I feared ending up with an angry husband. I worked hard to avoid guys who seemed like they had an angry side. I thought that if I appeared competent, independent, and respectful, I would be less likely to disappoint the guys I dated. Thus, men weren't often seeing my vulnerable and more emotional side. And I did not have a lot of respect or admiration for the men I chose to date.

As I continued to read Thomas's book, the Lord empowered me to confess to Him my most current fears about marriage. I began to release my fear of rejection, my fear of my being bored, my fear of divorce, and my fear of being undesired. I began to instead embrace the truth that I was a woman with an open, eager, and trusting heart. I said yes to what I most wanted: union with a strong, tender, honest, curious, stable, and passionate man of God. My heart was open to wonder, surprise, and a lasting marriage full of love. I welcomed being beloved and chosen. I began to envision what the fulfillment of love in my life would look like. I imagined my future husband and myself in the kitchen, laughing as we cooked a salmon dinner with local and organic vegetables, which we bought that evening at our downtown farmers market. I also saw us attentively listening to each other, worshiping God together, and going on grand adventures sailing to places like Italy, Australia, and Greece.

After reading *Calling in "The One,"* I pondered this question: "What would I have to give up in order to manifest this vision of love?"[3] I realized I would have to release the negative things that were holding me back and blocking my view of the man that God had for me. These negative things included my doubts that I would ever be loved by an amazing and godly man and my jealousy toward other people's seemingly ideal marriages.

In February 2010, two months before meeting Stephen, after reading the final chapter of *Calling in "The One,"* I heard God inviting me to be bold and ask for what I most wanted. Thus, my intention statement became *I will be dating my future husband by my 35th birthday.* My 35th birthday was just around the corner, only four-and-a-half months away, as many people reminded me.

For years, if I was at the grocery store or a friend's birthday party, it was normal for me to immediately scan the area for available cute and single guys. After feeling empowered by the Spirit of God to pray this bold prayer, I was even more alert and available to meeting someone.

One afternoon at a farmer's market, I found myself repeatedly walking past a certain young man selling produce. Suddenly, I realized that I desperately needed the tomatoes and squash that only his farm sold. We lingered talking, and I found myself staring at his six-foot-two frame, his unique hat, and his beautifully clear light blue eyes. He did look a lot younger than me, but he couldn't be that young, right? He wanted to hang out. So did I. He got my number. I had given my number to hot guys before, but I found myself getting more excited than usual internally wondering, "Is this it? Is *he* the answer to this wild and courageous prayer?"

Farmer boy ended up never calling. This guy, like many guys, looked intriguing and said all the right things, but he did not passionately pursue my heart.

My biggest doubt was wondering if someone would want to commit to *me* for life. Even as I doubted, I sensed Jesus reassuring me that my future husband would be captivated by me. I desperately wanted to believe this truth.

I also began to relearn that a man desiring me and wanting to spend the rest of his life with me is not what makes me worthy. I am already worthy. I pray that I always remember that my partner or work performance doesn't give me my identity.

Christ also taught me that we become intimate with those we pray to, those we pray for, and those we pray with. I heard God whispering in my spirit, "I'm building intimacy between you and your future husband, and I have been for years." Wow! No wonder it was such a coming home and intimate experience meeting Stephen.

A month and a half before meeting Stephen, I was encouraged to check out the website of the Sapphire Leadership Group, formerly Plumbline Ministry.[4] As I began to listen to their materials online regarding singleness, I was challenged to look at the history of my relationships and ask myself, "What doesn't match up and make sense?" As I've already mentioned, I was attracting weak and passive men, men who didn't have strong faith in God. This didn't make any sense because I was deeply passionate about my relationship with Jesus. Arthur Burke, an instructor from the aforementioned ministry, teaches that our forefathers' actions can affect us. At his instruction, I began to ask myself the following questions: "Am I carrying a label? Am I projecting in my spirit an iniquity from the past?" I asked God to reveal to my heart the sins in my family line two to three generations back. As I prayed, I heard the words *promiscuity, adultery, divorce, sexual abuse, bitterness, anger,* and *ungodliness.*

Later that day I wrote in my journal:

> *Lord, I sense that one of the reasons godly men have not been drawn to me is because of the sins of my ancestors. I've had the label of UNGODLY on me. Jesus, please remove this label and put a new name on my spirit so that godly men would see me, be curious about me, and ultimately pursue me.*

Arthur Burke went on to say that sometimes people we've dated in the past can put a label on us, a label saying that "we're already taken and no longer available." I initially didn't think that this applied to me, but as I sat in silence and waited on God, an ex-boyfriend's name was highlighted in my mind. This man was one of the first guys I ever dated, and, in my mind, it was a fairly positive and innocent relationship. Nonetheless, I sensed that this boyfriend had labeled me "taken." So, I prayed,

> *Lord, please remove this label that says, "I am already taken." Please declare in the spiritual realm that I am ready and available for courtship and love with an amazing and godly man.*

I was also encouraged to review lies and vows I'd believed. God highlighted for me lies and vows that He had already broken off over the years, such as "My parents weren't happy in their marriage, and I won't be happy either." Another lie was "I won't marry until my mom remarries and until certain single friends get married."

Plumbline Ministry also had a teaching on their website about jealousy and singlehood, which deeply resonated with me. I confessed my envy to God. I no longer wanted to be burdened by jealousy. The Lord then encouraged me to pray a prayer of thanksgiving and blessing over all my married family and friends. God showed me that He is never limited, and there's no shortage of the good gifts He has for us. For example, God's resources are not too limited to bless me with a husband and also bless all my friends and family with spouses.

Here are the positive affirmations I proclaimed out loud daily during those final months of being single:

My future husband focuses on and pursues me. He has the fruit of the Spirit (love, joy, peace . . .) in which he blesses me.

I am a fortunate and grateful woman of God, and I fully share in the abundant life of Jesus Christ with my beloved husband.

Eighteen days before meeting Stephen, I journaled:

The Lord does have a wonderful husband for me that He will unite me with. Worshipping God will be the central activity of our life. We will praise God as we sing and live out our lives with faith and gratitude. Christ encourages me not to fear and not to kill desire. The wait is almost over. Jesus will make the path clear. Christ has a life of beauty and play in store for us.

You know what I need, Lord. Guide me and let my roots be planted wherever is best for me. You alone know whether that's in Denver, Los Angeles, Seattle . . . You will empower me to trust you. You know what's best for me, Lord.

For Reflection:

1. Describe your dating pattern.
2. Ask Jesus to reveal to you any lies you've believed about love and marriage.
3. Ask Christ: What are You inviting me to release? What are You inviting me to embrace?
4. Wait on God to give you positive affirmations that you can focus on during this season in your life.

CHAPTER 5

What if your future husband doesn't live in Seattle?

Rebecca Reflects:

About a month before I met my future husband, my dad and stepmom came to visit me in Seattle. It's hard to describe exactly how God brought my dad healing in his life—and, in turn, brought my dad and me closer together. Growing up, my dad had always taught my brothers and me that God loved us, but it was a truth that he says he never truly received for himself. He described himself as angry, perfectionistic, and legalistic when we were kids. Thankfully, God's love and grace grabbed hold of my dad, and he began to be transformed. When I was in my midtwenties, my dad stopped trying to perform for God in order to receive love. From then on, he became more humble and teachable, and my heart became more open to spend time with him. My dad would learn new truths about God's unconditional love and grace, and about how God invites His children to live under His new covenant. Then he would passionately share what he was learning with me.

During their visit my dad challenged me with these words: "I know you love Seattle, Beb (family nickname), but what if your future husband doesn't live here?"

His words infuriated me. Didn't he know how much I loved Seattle? I had finally found a place I wanted to lay down roots, and I did not want to leave. Over the next few weeks, however, I began to ask myself, *Do I love Seattle more than I love God's plan for my life?* I hate to admit that this was not an easy question for me to answer. As I wrestled with this, I journaled:

> *Am I holding on to Seattle too tightly? Am I limiting myself and not accepting all that God has for me? Lord, I confess the ways Seattle has become an idol. I want to love my future husband more than I love the "Emerald City." Jesus, You're reminding me that I'm at home in your love, no matter where I live. I don't want to be afraid. Jesus, give me the courage I need to be open to all that You have for me.*

Over the next few weeks, as I spent time taking walks with God along the rocky beach near my apartment, the Lord began, as only He can, to open up my heart and deepen my ability to trust Him—so much so that I even began to pray that I'd be open to meeting men who lived outside of Seattle. One day as I was praying, the name of a man I'd met a few months back on eHarmony came to my mind. Originally, I had dismissed him because he lived in Denver, Colorado. Feeling challenged by my father's words, I contacted him. I took it a step further and let him know that I was coming to Denver in a few weeks for a work conference and asked if he would like to get together. During our brief interactions, he struck me as bright, creative, dependable, athletic, adventurous, and full of strong faith in God. I was intrigued and excited to meet him in person.

Because I didn't go to Colorado that often, I decided to spend a few days with my dad and stepmom in Colorado Springs before attending the conference. Our times together are always spiritually enriching, and they're both goofy and light-hearted so we laugh a lot together as well. My last day in Colorado Springs, they convinced me to babysit their "full of life" golden retriever, Theo. I'm not a dog person. I'm working on becoming one for my future kids' sake, as kids seem to love dogs. Babysitting and walking Theo ended up being a lot of fun, and Theo was so appreciative of any affection I offered him. I also got to meet new people who were drawn in by his lovable friendliness. After one of my walks with my new canine companion, as I sat journaling at a coffee house, I began to hear, almost in a whisper, the following words:

Your life is about to change FOREVER.

As I wrote these words down, I knew that Jesus was the One speaking to me, and I pondered what these words could mean. Perhaps God was referring to the bonding that had just happened between Theo and me. Maybe I had finally become a dog person and would never be the same again. Or, perhaps this was about my upcoming date with eHarmony guy. Was I *finally* about to meet my future husband!?

Stephen Reflects:

At thirty-eight years old and still single, I had reached a point in my life where I felt somewhat fulfilled. I had just started a private counseling practice in Colorado. My mission was to partner with God to bring healing to people's hearts and set them free to be all that God had created them to be. Months earlier, I had gone on a trip to Senegal, West Africa, with a close friend who had grown up there. I loved the experience. I was also excited about my involvement in a local ministry to men called Warriors at Heart. I had shared my life story at a breakfast two weeks before meeting Rebecca. After I spoke, the leader of the ministry put his arm around me and prayed that God would provide a woman for me. With all of this going on, I felt a deep sense of fulfillment and gratitude to God for my life. Yet, I still desired a wife. I was determined, however, not to settle for just anyone. I promised myself that I was going to pursue Christ to the best of my ability and step into wherever He led me.

With this mind-set, I left on April 22nd for a counseling conference in Denver. As I walked into the hotel where the conference was being held, the facilitator, Sarah, greeted me, "Hey, aren't you the guy who is engaged to . . .?"

"No," I said, "that's not me." I felt a little disappointed, wishing that I *were* engaged to someone.

I took my place in the front row next to a colleague. Thirty minutes later, three people walked in late. Sarah stopped, mid-lecture, and invited them to sit up front. The man replied, "My wife and I can sit up front, and my daughter can sit here in the back." At a break, I introduced myself to the man. "What is your counseling specialty?" I asked.

"I'm a Christian sex therapist," he said with a smile on his face. I laughed a good hearty laugh because it was the first time I had met someone with these credentials. After talking with him for a few minutes, I could tell that he was a cool guy, and I was glad to have met him.

Sarah lectured all day. Don't get me wrong, what she was talking about was interesting, but listening to someone for six hours can get tiring. So, to stay awake, I got up and walked to the back of the room where I could stand and listen. Now, you must understand that most counselors are of the female persuasion. There were about forty females and six males at this conference. It was a fantastic place for a single guy like me. So I did what most single guys would do in my situation—I scanned the room checking out the women. My eyes stopped at the back of a young woman's head. She had beautiful, brown, flowing hair, like the "flocks of Gilead" that Solomon said about his love. She was a beautiful woman, and that's about as far as my thoughts went.

After the conference ended for the day, I found myself talking to the Christian sex therapist when the same beautiful woman came up. "I'd like you to meet my daughter, Rebecca," he said. "Rebecca, this is Stephen. He's a counselor too."

She smiled and said, "I'm trying to get my dad to leave because I have an eHarmony date I need to get to."

I watched Rebecca and her folks leave. I didn't have much time to dwell on our interaction because another woman walked up to me and said, "Hi, I'm Lucy. I hear you're from Grand Junction. Well, I moved there about a year ago with my husband and I am 'dying.' I'm used to the big city, and there is no culture there."

"Hey, I go to a church that has a pastor who is Princeton educated, and I'm part of a ballroom dance group," I replied. "Also, I have some really good friends who are from Senegal. There *is* culture in Grand Junction! I'll introduce you to some cool stuff if you want." Lucy was a bubbly, outgoing person, someone who I enjoyed right away. I went on to tell her that I had just started my own private counseling practice. I added, "I am committed to staying in Grand Junction for at least a year, but I would like to find a wife, and if I don't find one, then I may need to move." Lucy and I said goodnight, and I left for the evening. I went to my friend's place where I was staying, feeling a little sad about being single.

Rebecca Reflects:

That first day at the conference I was experiencing renewed freedom from God to be more of who He had created *me* to be. The counseling conference emphasized experiential learning, and we practiced using the protocol and techniques with each other. My partner for that first session sensed that something big was coming up in my life. I resonated with his hunch. After all, I believed God had just told me that my life was about to change forever. I excitedly let my partner know that perhaps all of this was regarding my upcoming date that evening.

As I left the conference, my dad introduced me to a guy named Stephen, who had been sitting in the front row next to him and my stepmom. As we headed to the car, my stepmom asked, "So what did you think of that Stephen guy? Pretty cute, eh?" I just nodded. I didn't have time to think too much about her question. I wanted to quickly get back to the hotel to freshen up for my eHarmony date, who was on his way. I *had* noticed Stephen earlier in the day, and I'd been strangely drawn to the back of his head. But I dismissed it.

Seeing my eHarmony date in person was a bit of a shock. In his profile pictures, his hair was hidden by athletic hats and bike helmets. But now I was able to see his hairstyle, which was more suitable for the 80s than today. Let's just say there were lots of shaved parts mixed in with longer parts (think wanna-be mullet)—not the best combination.

He took me to a pizza parlor where he quickly became engrossed in a hockey game on the big screen. Not my idea of an ideal first date. A live hockey game would have been a different story. During dinner, all of a sudden my stomach felt queasy and tied in knots. I became so uncomfortable that I had to lay down flat on my back in the booth before I was able to get up to leave. Because I wondered if the TV and my getting sick contributed to our lack of connecting, I agreed to a second date for the following night.

Stephen Reflects:

The next morning at the conference, I sat in my usual seat. I was reading through my notes from the previous day when, out of the corner of my eye, I saw Rebecca's stepmom push Rebecca (the beautiful, brown-haired, "I have an eHarmony date" woman) toward me.

Rebecca tapped me on the shoulder and inquired, "May I sit here?"

I calmly and coolly replied, "Yes" (inside, I was like, *Yeah, baby!*).

So here I was, sitting next to this beauty, unaware of how my life was about to change forever. The instructor asked for alumni participants to partner up with newbie participants. She had the alumni come to the front of the room. Rebecca went up to the front, and a few minutes later, I went up and asked her if she wanted to be partners. Her reply was, "Why didn't you ask me to be your partner while I was still sitting next to you?"

She is a feisty one, I thought to myself. Despite her feistiness, we still partnered up. Rebecca became the "counselor," and I became her "client." Rebecca prayed for God's healing and leading. It was quickly apparent that God was guiding our time. God highlighted that when I was around thirteen or fourteen years old, I had believed a lie from the evil one. I had believed that any decision I made would have negative consequences; thus I felt paralyzed whenever I had to make decisions. At the time, I was trying to decide whether I should attend a Christian high school where my brother and best friend had transferred to. It was a difficult decision because to change schools would mean I would be leaving many people I cared about. During this prayer time with Rebecca, things became crystal clear, because up to this point, at age thirty-eight, decisions (small and great) were incredibly difficult for me. I started weeping. I was sad for all that the enemy had taken, but I was also glad that this lie and agreement were being broken and that God was bringing His healing to me. I was sobbing uncontrollably at this point.

Rebecca, with a twinkle in her eye, jokingly responded to me, "Don't snot on me. I don't want to get sick. I have a hot date tonight!"

During this intense healing, I *really* noticed Rebecca's heart. Her beauty was stunning, and it literally pierced my heart. Her physical beauty, combined with her compassion and tenderness toward me, overwhelmed me. God was giving me a glimpse into her heart. She was a beautiful, compassionate, fun, and powerful woman. I found myself deeply attracted to her, more than I had ever felt toward any woman before. On top of this, I suddenly heard God speak in a still, small voice to my heart: "Stephen, she is My gift to you!"

I stopped Rebecca in the middle of the session and asked, "Rebecca, when are you going back to Seattle?"

She replied, "Monday. Why?"

"May I take you out on a date on Sunday?"

Rebecca, apparently a little flustered, shyly nodded, "Yes." After this, Rebecca lost her focus, and we needed to call over one of the facilitators to finish the session.

Rebecca Reflects:

As I prayed for Stephen, I was overcome by Christ's compassion for him. It was apparent how much our Creator loved and cared for this man. It was an honor to witness God healing Stephen and opening him up to new possibilities in his life. I had the sense that somehow *I* was to be involved in all the healing that God was doing in Stephen's heart.

Later my partner from the first day of the conference and his wife checked in. "So how'd your date go?"

"Uh, it was just okay. I didn't feel a strong connection with him. I'm wondering if the healing God did yesterday was about preparing me to meet someone else."

My partner nodded, and with a smile he said, "I know. I think it involves him," and he pointed to Stephen.

Grinning, I replied, "That's interesting. Stephen did just ask me out on a date for tomorrow night."

That Saturday afternoon, after working with Stephen, I couldn't eat lunch (and I love to eat). My brain felt like it was cotton candy floating far away into the clouds. During an afternoon break, my dad, stepmom, and I went back to the hotel room. I was nervously pacing in our living room. I didn't know what was happening. I had never felt so undone. My stepmom wisely encouraged me to pause and take some time to myself to rest and talk with the Lord about how I was feeling. As I cried out to the Lord, I became aware that He had planted huge amounts of love in my heart for a man that I had just met the night before. Stephen was a "stranger" to me, and yet it was like my spirit already knew him and felt connected to him. I couldn't wait to see his handsome face again, hear his deep, sexy voice, and get to know *everything* I could about him. I had never before been so intrigued by a man, and so interested in being a part of what God was doing in his life.

Stephen Reflects:

After working with Rebecca, I had to get outside and gain some composure because I had been weeping so much. I went outside and walked in the beautiful grounds of the Denver Tech Center for two hours, skipping lunch. Skipping a meal is a big deal for me, because rarely do I miss a meal on purpose. I love to eat! During this time alone, I prayed and asked God what was going on.

After gaining some composure, I went back inside, sat down next to Rebecca, and tried to listen to the instructor. At the next break, I walked up to Rebecca's father and said, "Um, I know this is a bit old school, but I asked your daughter out on a date a few hours ago, and I want to ask you for your permission."

Her dad responded with a smile, "Rebecca left home when she was seventeen years old. She can make up her own mind what she wants to do." It was apparent, however, that he felt honored to be a part of what was unfolding.

Later that afternoon, Rebecca's stepmom called me over and said to the woman she was talking to, "Lucy, you need to tell Stephen what you just told me."

Lucy (who I just met the previous day) hesitated for a moment and then said, "Stephen, this doesn't happen to me much, but God woke me up early this morning, and I was impressed to pray for you. Specifically, I prayed that you would meet your future wife."

I dropped my head in bewilderment, thinking to myself, *What the heck is going on?* At this point, I started crying again.

As the seminar was winding down for the day, I turned to Rebecca and confessed, "I don't know what is going on, but I am feeling extremely drawn to you."

"I know. I am feeling drawn to you as well," Rebecca admitted. "Unfortunately, I am committed to another date tonight."

"No problem; yeah, you should keep your commitment. Here is my phone number, though, just in case you get back early and want to hang out."

At the end of the day, I walked Rebecca, her dad, and her stepmom out to their car. Rebecca did not even look at me. I just figured she was focused on her date. I was glad that I had a date lined up with her for the following night. I called and left a message for a friend back home and excitedly requested, "Please pray for me, because I believe God has led me to my future wife."

I drove back to my friend's house in Denver. He poured me a glass of Merlot, which I raised and announced, "I would like to make a toast to my future wife, Rebecca Fuller, whom I just met today!" We both laughed, and I told him the story of the day. We settled in for our planned guys' night, which included dinner, beer, and watching a Lakers' play-off basketball game. At halftime, I started making plans for my date with Rebecca. I settled on a short hike, dinner, and swing dancing at the Mercury Café in downtown Denver.

Rebecca Reflects:

Meanwhile, as I got ready for my second date with eHarmony guy, my heart was pounding because of all that had happened between Stephen and me earlier that day. In the elevator on the way to meet my date, I encountered a petite woman who looked to be in her seventies. Because her face was full of such love and kindness, I boldly blurted out with panic in my voice, "Are you a praying woman?" When she replied yes, I quickly whispered, "I have guy trouble." She responded with a knowing look. A look that told me, "I'm on it." It was such a calming experience that I have since wondered if she was an angel sent from heaven to shower me with God's peace.

I met my date in the hotel lobby and immediately explained that I had undergone a lot of personal healing at the conference. I said I was emotionally drained and, unfortunately, didn't know how good of company I'd be that evening. This was true, and it felt kinder than saying, "I met this guy named Stephen . . . fireworks are going off in my heart. I think he's the one!"

I suggested that we just grab coffee at a local coffee shop. I wanted to get back early enough to call Stephen. Our weekend was almost over, and I hoped to spend as much time as possible getting to know him.

I was a bit annoyed that my date decided to take me forty-five minutes across town to his favorite coffee shop. As he opened the coffee shop door, loud Middle Eastern music greeted us, as well as belly dancers, who were in the middle of a dance performance. I love dancing and enjoyed the unexpected performance. My date, on the other hand, seemed extremely uncomfortable; his face was scrunched up and constipated like a prune. He was doing everything in his power to avoid looking at the dancers' alluring smiles and exposed midriffs. I marveled at how skilled they were at doing graceful, powerful wavelike movements with their hips. I wondered if he felt it would be a sin to enjoy their dance performance.

Even though I wanted our date to be on the shorter side, I did not want to leave with any regrets. After all, I *had* been originally intrigued during our initial e-mail interactions.

I wanted to quickly learn more about this man's relationship with God, and so I began with, "I love that Jesus is always speaking to us about how much He loves us."

He responded with, "What do you mean God speaks? Have you recently heard God's audible voice? We already have His Holy Scriptures, which clearly communicates His perfect plan for the world."

"Yes," I replied. "The Bible is God's love letter to us. But, I also hear God's voice as I'm gazing at a beautiful sunset, or listening to music, or out to lunch with a friend. Jesus is creatively pursuing and wooing our hearts into a deeper relationship with Himself. He is an amazing God. A God of beauty and redemptive miracles..."

He interrupted with, "You have a highly romantic view of who you want God to be. Christ is not the casual God you make Him out to be. Miracles and signs and wonders ended in biblical times."

This man did not believe God still communicated and is actively involved in our lives. I desired to be with a partner who would want to talk to God about every detail of our lives, from seeking God's guidance in buying a new car, to praying about when to start trying to have children. He went on to explain in detail his mission to defend the Judeo-Christian faith. After we talked, I felt like I was on trial and that he was not so sure that I belonged in the kingdom of God.

During our conversation, I noticed that he wasn't looking me in the eye. I didn't have anything to lose, so I asked point-blank, "It seems like you're working hard to avoid looking at me. Are you uncomfortable talking face to face?"

He answered me matter-of-factly, "Yes, I am. We should go for a drive."

I had asked to meet his dog (Frodo, a collie) at some point, but I was quite surprised to find that he brought him along for both of our dates. At one point, we drove past his house, and then he pulled over to a nearby park where he did some Frisbee tricks with Frodo. Then he announced, "Well, that's all I got—my house and my dog. That's what I have to offer a woman." I prayed he was joking. His comments revealed potential insecurity and lack of confidence on his part. Also, his love for his dog was touching, but I wondered if he had room in his life for another love besides Frodo.

Back in the car, Frodo tried to sneak from the backseat to the front. My date commented, "Move, Frodo. Rebecca and I are talking."

I almost laughed and wanted to say, "Actually, Frodo, your dad is talking, talking *at* me. He doesn't really need or seem to want my input in the conversation." Normally, I would find this behavior rude and upsetting. In this instance, I was thankful for the space to take some deep breaths and process all that had happened earlier in the day with Stephen.

Finally, it looked like we were making our way back to my hotel. On the way, we passed a herd of buffalo on the side of the road. "Wow, I've never seen buffalo before!" I exclaimed.

"Really?" he said, pulling the car over. "You should take a closer look."

I was sorry I'd mentioned it, because he insisted that we get out and take numerous pictures. Then he was adamant that I just couldn't pass by the Red Rocks Amphitheater without taking a peak. Unfortunately, it happened to be jam-packed because a prom was being held there that evening. Was this date ever going to end?

We finally pulled into the entrance to my hotel. With his car engine still running, he looked at me and said, "It must be humbling being a counselor, while still needing healing and having many issues of your own."

"Well, I'm a work in progress," I responded. "God is still healing me, and this weekend is about *my* personal healing and development. When I'm with my clients, though, it's all about them and their healing."

He replied in a matter-of-fact tone, "But even so, you do have *just* about all of the qualities I'm looking for, and I'd like to continue dating you."

"Thank you for our dates. You are a quality person, but I don't feel we are a good match for each other."

Even though eHarmony guy and I ended up not being a great match, I am grateful for our interactions. God used them to open up my heart to the possibility of meeting someone who lived in Colorado.

My interactions with eHarmony guy were similar to interactions I've had with Christian guys over the years.

Many Christian men I've met are more comfortable living from their heads and not their hearts. This usually looks like the guy not being comfortable vulnerably sharing his emotions or being open to hearing about mine. One reason Stephen was so initially sexy to me was because he was confident enough in who he was as a man to cry in front of me, a woman he had just met. He wasn't trying to play it cool. During our interactions, I could tell that God's love was a powerful force in his life and that he lived life with his eyes open, open to be touched by the beauty and pain all around him. His heart was alive; he was not shut down like so many of the men I had known or dated. Stephen didn't strike me as someone who had everything already figured out in his life; he instead seemed teachable, curious, and eager to continue to learn and grow.

By the time my date had dropped me off at my hotel, it was already 9:00 p.m. As I pondered whether it was too late to call Stephen, my father and stepmother chimed in, "Call him. He'll be thrilled to hear from you!" It was a bit intense having my dad and stepmom so involved in our unfolding love story. Nonetheless, their prayers and encouragement were ultimately appreciated. And it was fun to all be getting to know Stephen at the same time.

Stephen Reflects:

Meanwhile, back at guys' night in, my phone rang.

"Hi, this is Rebecca. I just got home from my date. Would you like to hang out?"

Excitedly and nervously, I replied, "Ah, yeah, I'll be right over." I told my friend that he was on his own. On the way to Rebecca's hotel, I was compelled to pull over and get a dozen red roses. Looking back, I really think God was coaching me because I had never given a woman a dozen roses, let alone on the first day I had met her. I greeted Rebecca at the elevator with the roses. I thought to myself, "She is gorgeous!"

I opened the car door for her, and we sped off under the curious gaze of her father. We headed to Maggiano's, a classy Italian restaurant. Neither of us were hungry, so we decided to take a walk around the Denver Tech Center grounds. After an enjoyable walk, we entered the restaurant, where we were led to a booth that reminded me of a spot an Italian godfather might sit in. It was a big horseshoe-shaped booth that could seat about eight people, and it was raised up above the other tables. Rebecca and I soaked in the atmosphere, chatting with our waiter and getting to know each other. Soon, we found ourselves next to each other in the "Godfather" booth, with my arm draped around Rebecca's shoulders. We both looked at each other and wondered, how did "this" all happen?

Rebecca playfully punched me and anxiously pronounced, "Yeah, but I live in Seattle and you live in Colorado—and I am not moving. How is this going to work?"

"Let's not worry about all that," I said calmly. "Let's just enjoy the moment and the time we have together."

After I dropped off Rebecca that night, I was filled with such joy and excitement that I could barely sleep. I remember praying and thanking God for what it appeared He was doing. The next day, I arrived at the conference, and Rebecca was nowhere to be found. Her stepmom told me, "Don't worry about Rebecca. I think she's in the other room doing a relaxation exercise. As you know, this has been an eventful weekend."

Rebecca Reflects:

That morning my feet weren't touching the ground and my stomach was gurgling with a mixture of joy and anxiety. I did not feel ready to see Stephen just yet. I felt like I needed more space to catch my breath. I decided to call my mom and fill her in on all the latest exciting news. The relationship I have with her is a treasured gift. During our time together in Seattle we often prayed, with great anticipation and hope, for my future husband and marriage, and we had fun dreaming about every little detail of my future wedding day. With joy in her voice, she prayed for me, and

I felt God's peace and calm fill my heart. I finally rejoined the conference about an hour later.

Stephen Reflects:

During the conference that day, we both decided that it was not a good idea to partner up again. But, we definitely kept our eyes on each other. I wrote her a note after being away from her for thirty minutes: "I MISSED YOU!"

Later that day, I had lunch with Rebecca and her family. I was amazed at how quickly I felt connected to them. While at lunch, I got a text from my dad, affectionately known as "Pops," telling me that my brother got kicked out of a basketball game he was coaching for my nephews who were eleven and nine years old. My brother didn't like some of the calls the refs were making. Pops ended by saying, "The cops were called!" I read this text message and laughed to myself, wondering what Rebecca would think of *my* crazy family.

After lunch, during a break, I was walking to the back of the room when Sarah, the head facilitator, came up the aisle toward me. She stopped me, leaned in, and whispered in my ear, "Work it! Work it!" It was then that I realized that Rebecca and I were being watched by many of the women in the room. They were witnessing, and apparently enjoying, the unfolding romance. I just shook my head and laughed as I walked out the door.

Rebecca Reflects:

Stephen took me to Ted's Montana Grill, near the 16th Street Mall in downtown Denver. As Stephen prayed before we ate dinner, I knew that this was the man I'd been waiting for all my life. I don't remember the words of Stephen's prayer exactly, but as we held hands, I felt loved, cared about, and safer than I'd ever felt before. Our spirit-to-spirit connection was amazing! I had always been skeptical of people who experienced love so quickly. God continued to give confirmation, reminding me that intimacy had already been built between Stephen and me through our years of praying for each other. When we finally met, intimacy was already there. As I ate dinner with Stephen, I felt relaxed. I didn't have to perform or pretend to be somebody I wasn't. He seemed to be enjoying getting to know the real me. Conversation flowed freely and naturally, and it was nice to know that we had each other's full attention. Like our first date, we found ourselves sitting closer and closer as the night went on. I knew in my heart that we belonged together. It was truly a coming home experience just being with him.

Stephen Reflects:

We lingered over a delicious meal, enjoying getting to know each other and gazing into each other's eyes. Toward the end of our meal, Rebecca got a call from her father. He informed us that it was snowing and they were going only twenty miles per hour heading down to their home in Colorado Springs. It was late, and Rebecca and I had no desire to drive in the dark and the snow. We decided to make the trip in the morning.

We ended up spending the night at a close friend's house—Rebecca in one room and me in another room. It was really cool because Rebecca was able to meet a good friend of mine and his wife. She was able to see that I had at least one good friend. Maybe, I wasn't a "crazy" guy after all!

We enjoyed a good night's sleep and headed off to Colorado Springs the next morning so Rebecca could catch her flight back to Seattle. It was a beautiful Rocky Mountain day with freshly fallen snow sparkling under the blue, sunny Colorado sky. Rebecca and I were so wrapped up in talking, the scenery, the music, and each other that we failed to realize that her father had been trying to call us. As we pulled into the driveway, we were listening to the love song "Fallin' for You" by Colbie Caillat. She was singing our story:

> *I don't know what to do; I think I'm falling for you,*
>
> *I've been waiting all my life and now I've found you,*
>
> *I don't know what to do; I think I'm falling for you.*

Oh, I just can't take it, my heart is racing.

We greeted her dad and stepmom, and Rebecca got on the computer to confirm her flight's departure time. Suddenly, she exclaimed, "I can't believe it. I missed my flight!" She had mistakenly thought that her flight was leaving at 1:00 p.m., but it was actually getting into Seattle at 1:00 p.m. Her flight had already left! We all wondered how this could have happened. Perhaps she was a bit distracted—by love.

I needed to get back to Grand Junction for work that night, so I regretfully started saying my good-byes to Rebecca. Her dad and stepmom gave us our space, but her dad was sneaking in to see if we were going to kiss—we think. I wanted to kiss Rebecca, but instead I leaned in and said, "I think we should wait to kiss." She reluctantly agreed.

Her dad then asked me if I could give him a ride up to Denver. He was attending Monday classes at Denver Seminary, and he didn't want to leave his wife without a car for the day. I said, "Sure, no problem."

Within minutes of leaving the house, he turned to me with a big grin and inquired, "So, how is it going?"

I laughed and answered, "Great. Mr. Fuller. Uh, should I call you Bill or Mr. Fuller?"

"You can call me Bill."

"Well, Bill, I want to marry your daughter!"

"Oh, is that so?" he replied with a serious look on his face. "Well, then, do you mind if I ask you a few questions?"

"No, not at all. You can ask whatever questions you like. I have nothing to hide."

So, for the entire hour-and-fifteen-minute car ride from Colorado Springs to Denver, Rebecca's Christian sex therapist father grilled me. He did not hold back. He asked many personal questions, as only a Christian-sex-therapist father of an only daughter might ask. Needless to say, it was a very long ride to Denver!

Rebecca Reflects:

As Dad and Stephen drove to Denver, my stepmom and I headed to the airport. I panicked because I had to be at work in Seattle the following morning. As we approached the ticket counter, I plopped down my gorgeous red roses and heaved a big sigh. I pointed at my ticket, but audible words didn't come out.

My stepmom took over. "My stepdaughter has missed her flight to Seattle. Look at her; she is so obviously in *love* and is not thinking clearly right now! Is there any way we can get her on another flight to Seattle?" Thankfully, the ticket counter attendant graciously waved the rebooking fees, got me on a flight to Seattle the next morning, and seemed genuinely pleased to hear about my newfound love.

Later that night, I asked my father how badly he had grilled Stephen. My dad nonchalantly replied, "What's the big deal? I just asked Stephen about his complete sexual history and about any sexual addictions he currently has." I was mortified because I knew that he was telling the truth!

When Stephen and I talked, I was amazed to hear him say, "Your dad loves you so much, and he has every right to grill me." I was impressed with how much he appreciated my dad. He was confident and completely willing to be open and honest about his life. The mature way he handled my dad's questions made me respect him even more.

Stephen Reflects:

When Rebecca's dad and I finally arrived at Denver Seminary, I sheepishly inquired, "Well, Bill, do I still have your permission to pursue your daughter?"

Bill replied, "Actually, I would be glad if you did."

I then asked Bill if he had any suggestions for me as to how to pursue Rebecca. He recommended that we read together the book *Love and War* by John and Stasi Eldredge. In addition, he challenged me to pursue her heart. He then placed his hand on the back of my head and prayed a prayer of blessing over me and Rebecca. It was a very sacred moment! I walked back to my car in tears. As I drove the four hours through the Rocky Mountains back to my home, I was in awe and filled with joy over what had happened that weekend. I sent my Pops a text: "I am going to marry this girl!" His reply was, "We all want details. Call immediately!"

For Reflection:

1. Is getting married a desire of your heart? If so, ask God to give you courage to step out in faith and let go of any control you're holding on to regarding how it will all unfold.
2. If you are married, write down words or images describing your love story. If your love story were made into a movie, what would it be titled?
3. Write about a significant "coming home" experience you've had.

CHAPTER 6

I want to marry you

Stephen Reflects:

I arrived home Monday evening, and the next day I sent Rebecca an e-mail. "I know this is crazy and I don't want to scare you away, but I know I want to marry you! I want to protect you, provide for you, take care of you, have children with you, walk with God with you, build God's Kingdom with you, and make love to you!"

Let me remind you that this was written and sent via e-mail on Tuesday, four days after meeting Rebecca. In hindsight, this was not the most romantic venue for expressing these feelings.

Rebecca Reflects:

I didn't read Stephen's e-mail till around midnight the day he sent it. I am so glad my roommate was a night owl, as I'm a verbal processor. I immediately started weeping and laughing. I felt out of control with my intense emotions. She prayed and asked Christ to center me and give me space to catch my breath. Then we laughed some more and rejoiced through our tears. She had witnessed, firsthand, each precious detail of our unfolding love story. Also, a few months before meeting Stephen, she had a dream that I met someone on one of my upcoming trips. He and I lived in different states, and we quickly married. Wow, how prophetic and true her dream turned out to be!

Stephen Reflects:

The morning after I sent the e-mail, I told a friend about what I had done. "I felt exposed, a little foolish, scared," I said, "but even so, my heart is alive!" That evening Rebecca and I talked, and she sounded uncomfortable: "Your words were a lot, Stephen. I need to sit with what you said. Can we take a little break? Your emotions are so strong and clear, and I need a few days to check in with myself and see how I'm feeling about everything."

It was difficult to slow down, but I wanted to respect Rebecca's wishes. I didn't call Rebecca for a couple of days.

Then on Friday, sometime in the afternoon, I got a call from . . . guess who? Rebecca told me that after pondering everything, she was angry because she felt like I "ruined everything" by declaring my love too soon. But she had gotten over it because she remembered that she had been praying for someone just like me, someone who would passionately pursue her heart and put himself out there.

When I told a newer friend about meeting Rebecca, he exclaimed, "Hey, I just booked a trip out to Seattle to visit my brother. Stephen, you should fly out with me and visit Rebecca."

I casually replied, "Good idea; I will." The day I booked my flight to Seattle, Rebecca had already booked her flight to visit me the following month in Grand Junction.

After working in my basement one Saturday afternoon, I wrote in my journal:

> *I am extremely motivated to get the basement fixed up now, so it can be ready for Rebecca. I feel like God's blessings are all over me! It is amazing! The other day I was remodeling my basement. I was all alone and I had to stop and weep because of the thought of Rebecca and God's goodness to me!*

On my way to the airport, my dad texted me, "Have a great time in Seattle. Enjoy learning who Rebecca is. Relax with the knowledge God brought you both together. Let the game come to you."

This text was extra special to me because I deeply treasured our restored relationship. In my early years, I had longed for him to teach me about life. I had also desired for him to instruct me how to love a woman. All these things I had to learn on my own. So for Pops to send me a text like this spoke of the redemption of our hearts and our relationship. I quietly pondered his words and felt deep gratitude and joy well up in my soul.

I flew out to Seattle with my new friend. We changed planes in Denver, and I dragged him through the Denver airport so I could buy a dozen red roses for my beloved. I got the roses, but then we almost missed the plane to Seattle because we unexpectedly had to go back through security. We made it to our plane with minutes to spare. I told my friend that it was worth it because women love flowers. And as we entered the plane, all the flight attendants made comments about the roses and joked with me by thanking me for the flowers. One attendant said, "Here, I'll take these for you and make sure they are well taken care of." My friend glanced back at me, and I gave him an "I told you so" look. He just smiled and continued on to his seat.

After the three-hour flight, I reunited with Rebecca outside the baggage area. It was fantastic to be with her again—so surreal! Since it was late, Rebecca brought me directly to the friend's house where she had arranged for me to stay. Below is an excerpt of what I wrote in my journal the first night in Seattle:

> *It feels so good to see and be with Rebecca! It is tough to be apart from her just for the night. She is amazing . . . beautiful, love for God, spunky, fun . . . way cool!*

The next day she coyly posed a question to me, "Stephen, you wouldn't do anything without us talking about it, would you?" Inside, I was laughing because I knew that Rebecca thought I was going to propose to her during this visit. I was ready to marry Rebecca the day I met her, and a few days later I did express this to her via e-mail. (Remember how well that went over?) She asked me to slow down, which I had. And yes, I did still want to marry Rebecca. Despite all of this, no, I was not planning to propose to her that weekend. We both thought it wise and respectful for each of us to meet each other's families first before we moved forward.

I casually asked Rebecca, "What have you always envisioned regarding how you would get engaged?"

Rebecca replied, "I have always thought it would be fantastic to get engaged on a boat." I took this bit of information and tucked it away, until the time came to implement my plan.

Here is another journal entry:

> *Wonderful day with Rebecca! We took in some of the sights of Seattle such as the Pike Place Fish Market, Starbucks' first coffee shop, a park overlooking Seattle, and St. Mark's Cathedral. At St. Marks, Rebecca asked me to join her in doing a walking meditation through a labyrinth on the floor. She asked me to be open to giving any concerns over to God and walk along prayerfully. As I walked, I heard God speak to me, "Stephen, I am with you. I have always been with you. I will always be with you. You the man! She is my gift to you!" I met Rebecca in the center of the labyrinth, where she invited*

> *us to receive whatever Christ had for us. It was a powerful moment! I felt God's presence with us. I started to cry, being overwhelmed with God's goodness and blessing to me. Rebecca and I then held hands, prayed, and walked out together. Amazing!*

The next day, Rebecca offered to rub my feet. I politely protested, "No, thank you." You see, I love to have my feet rubbed, not that they have been rubbed much by anyone—ever. But, my feet, particularly my toenails, are extremely unattractive. My family has lovingly teased me for years about my toes and how gross they appear.

Nonetheless, Rebecca insisted that she rub my feet. "No" was not an option. She proceeded to give me a foot massage. It felt fantastic, but after about fifteen minutes, I started to cry as emotion welled up in me. Not only was she touching these ugly feet of mine, but I also thought about the many places my feet had been and seen. I sensed, at that moment, that Rebecca was experiencing some of that with me. It seemed like she was trying to know me on a deeper level. It was like she was literally touching my soul. I wept. I was speechless. Her tenderness toward me was overwhelming. I tried to share some of this with Rebecca, but it was difficult to put into words.

Rebecca's rubbing my feet was such an intimate experience. It gave me deeper insight and feeling for the story of Mary anointing Jesus' feet with oil. I had never before realized how intimate and humbling it is to have your feet washed and rubbed. Powerful! Spending time with Rebecca was more than I could have ever imagined. I enjoyed being with her and hearing her heart. I loved it. I loved this woman. I loved Rebecca Fuller and I wanted to marry her!

The next day my personal masseuse massaged my hands, back, and feet. Again, I started crying because it felt like God used her to touch my soul. We walked to downtown Edmonds and to the beach. While at the beach, I met Rebecca's mom via phone. It was fun to chat with her. I knew how close she and Rebecca were, and I looked forward to meeting her in person. Later that evening, Rebecca made me one of the best meals I have ever had: pistachio-encrusted salmon over spinach, roasted rosemary potatoes, thyme-scented asparagus, and a bottle of Merlot. It was delicious. The way to a man's heart is definitely through his stomach. I was hooked by this beautiful woman.

The following day, I flew back to western Colorado. I cried when I left her at the airport and, yet again, was left speechless. So I prayed silently for her. That morning, Rebecca had made me a phenomenal French toast breakfast and had prepared a lunch for my flight home. When the plane got up in the air, the clouds parted and I saw "The Mountain," Mount Rainier, for the first time. It was majestic. A text I sent to my Pops summed up the weekend well: "Pops, thanks for the advice. I let the game come to me. Fantastic weekend!"

For Reflection:

1. With whom are you able to share your heart?
2. Share about a time you felt called to serve another person and/or a time another person's tender love and care blessed you.
3. What has moved you to tears recently?

CHAPTER 7

I could never live in such a small town

Stephen Reflects:

Three weeks after my Seattle visit, Rebecca flew to visit me in Grand Junction. "Come to me, Beautiful," is what I texted Rebecca the day she flew in. Again, my Pops offered similar advice when he texted me, "Have a great time with Rebecca. Same game plan. You're doing great!" It was fun to pick up Miss Fuller at the tiny Grand Junction airport. I waited for her with a dozen red roses in my hand and with love, joy, and hope in my heart. I had a variety of things planned for Rebecca's trip. I was hoping that Western Colorado would display all of her glory for this special guest to make her feel welcome and at home. As it turned out, Rebecca did feel very much at home as it rained for the majority of the weekend, which is unusual for this part of the country.

Some of the highlights of this trip included watching the first game of the World Cup, taking private dance lessons, and enjoying appetizers at a fancy restaurant, with more dancing afterward.

Rebecca Reflects:

I was impressed that Stephen loved to dance and was thrilled to share one of my favorite activities with him. However, I think Stephen forgot our conversation over appetizers that Friday night at the fancy restaurant:

"Are you okay, Rebecca? You seem kind of quiet."

Long pause. "Yeah, I'm just taking it all in . . ." Another long pause. "I have to be honest with you, Stephen. I don't want to be hurtful, but the truth is I don't think I could live in such a small town—ever. You love it here, and I can tell you want to stay here. But, I love the city and Seattle, and I just don't know how this is all gonna work."

"Okay, what exactly are you saying?"

"I don't know. I want to be with you, but making it all work feels impossible. Maybe this just isn't gonna work." Long pause. "Maybe we need to end things."

Long pause. "Well, I think it would be a mistake to break up. And, I don't sense that's what you really want. I know it's not what I want. Let's just enjoy dancing tonight and your visit this weekend. Let's take things one step at a time and see what God has in store for us."

In light of this freak-out moment, I'm grateful for Stephen's calm response. His advice to take things step-by-step, as they came up in the moment, ended up being a wonderful plan for us.

Stephen Reflects:

This also happened to be the Saturday that a men's group I am a part of was holding their annual dinner to honor the women in their lives. It was fun to introduce Rebecca to some of the men from this ministry. While serenaded by live classical piano music, we all enjoyed a delicious meal, topped off with decadent chocolate mousse. The setting was a Western Colorado peach orchard.

Rebecca's dad and stepmom drove out from Colorado Springs to visit with us on Sunday. We attended church together, and I invited them back to my house for Cincinnati Chili. It was good to get to know them better, and they were glad to see Rebecca. I could see how much they loved her. During the meal, Rebecca's dad took a deep breath and posed the question, "So, how is it going between you two? Stephen, you live here in Colorado, and Rebecca, you live in Seattle. Have you guys talked about this?"

Rebecca was not pleased with this question, as her body language demonstrated. But it did help us talk about this important issue regarding our relationship—what would be done about the distance? After dinner, Rebecca's dad and stepmom asked if they could pray for us. In the middle of the prayer, Rebecca started crying. I thought, *finally!* Up to this point, I had been the only one crying in our relationship.

After they left, Rebecca and I enjoyed the rest of the evening together. I could sense that something had shifted in Rebecca. Until that evening, she had been adamant that she could never live in a small town like Grand Junction. There appeared to be a new openness in her heart. She suggested that we spend some time listening to the Bible on CD. While we were listening, I felt a strong desire to tell Rebecca that I loved her. However, many years ago, a wise man gave me advice that he had given to his sons. He said, "Never tell a woman you love her until you put a ring on her finger." I had taken this advice to heart, and other than the e-mail where I told Rebecca that I wanted to marry her, I had never before told a woman I loved her. I silently prayed and asked God for permission to tell Rebecca I loved her. Sensing that God was giving me the thumbs-up, I turned to Rebecca and professed, "I LOVE YOU!"

Her eyes got really big, and with a sigh of relief she confessed, "I have wanted to say that to you for a while now, but I have been waiting." I was thankful that she did wait and allowed me to initiate, which is what I was born to do. I believe God has made men to be the initiators and women as the responders; things seem to go better with this sort of dance.

Rebecca Reflects:

That Sunday afternoon during my dad and stepmom's prayer, I felt deeply loved by them both. As we prayed something shifted, and I was able to genuinely release my need for control. I surrendered to the Lord my doubts over the logistics and felt physically lighter. I was now able to take a deep breath, fully relax, and enjoy the present moment. Later I shared with a close friend how wonderful it was to close out that Sunday evening by listening to the book of Philippians on CD with Stephen.

Her response was, "Wow! Do you realize how rare it is to be with a guy who's willing to listen to the Bible on CD with you? You guys are a perfect match."

Hearing Stephen tell me he loved me left me feeling incredibly special. I felt both grounded and giddy. I had felt his love all along in his actions toward me, but to hear the words "I love you" out loud solidified everything. I had been eager to tell him that I loved him, but I'm glad he went first. The fact that he initiated our first date and shared his feelings with me first left me feeling secure, knowing that I was with a godly man who had the courage to lead and the courage to follow his heart. It told me that being with me is what he really wanted. It made me less likely to doubt his desire to be with me in the future.

For Reflection:

1. What do you think about the man being the initiator and the woman being the responder? Do you agree/disagree? Why?
2. Have you told dating partners that you've loved them? What are your thoughts about reserving this statement for your future spouse?
3. If you're currently in a dating relationship, or are engaged, ask God what He would like to say to you regarding your relationship.

CHAPTER 8

Don't come back 'til you find yourself

Stephen Reflects:

Every year for the past twelve years, most of my family has gathered in southeastern Michigan for a family reunion. My brother and his lovely wife have a beautiful lake house. Having grown up in New Jersey, my brother wanted to bring some of the uniqueness of the East Coast to the Midwest. Thus, he and my father developed the idea of flying out lobsters and grilling them for family and friends. The event was dubbed "Lobster Fest"! For the past twelve years, I have flown or driven from wherever I was living to attend Lobster Fest.

Adding excitement to Lobster Fest 2010 was the news that I was bringing Rebecca for the family to meet for the first time. This was a big deal, as many family members had encouraged me over the years to "hurry up and find a wife." In fact, the year before, my sister-in-law had thoroughly grilled me in front of other family members about that very topic. She wanted some more nieces and nephews, and she was tired of waiting for me, her thirty-seven-year-old bachelor brother-in-law.

Not surprisingly, it did not take long for the family to fall in love with Rebecca. At one point, my stepmother pulled me aside so she could personally sing Rebecca's praises. She easily fit in and was game for the constant activities at the lake: swimming, boating, water-skiing, tubing, biking, running, Wiffle ball, touch football, cards, and Baggo (Corn Hole). Our family and my sister-in-law's family took their game playing very seriously. In fact, one of the events was a double elimination Baggo tournament. Players were seeded according to ability. There were two groups: Level 1 and Level 2, with the Level 1 group being the best players and the Level 2 . . . not so much. Names were placed in a hat, and teams were drawn at random. The goal was to pair up a Level 1 player with a Level 2 player. As fate would have it, Rebecca was partnered with my extremely competitive brother. He has been known to throw his partner in the lake for not performing up to his standards. This was going to be quite interesting!

The Baggo tournament began, and everyone had their eyes on my brother to see how he would respond to Rebecca's Baggo playing. He initially appeared to be composed, supportive, and respectful of his partner, even though her Baggo game left much to be desired. The patriarch of my sister-in-law's clan leaned over to me, and with a glint in his eye, commented, "Wow, your brother seems to be on his best behavior." I nodded, knowingly, and silently wondered how long it would last. It did not last that long, as after one match (their first loss), my brother yelled, "Rebecca, don't come back until you've found yourself!"

When it was their turn to play again, Rebecca was nowhere to be found. After an extensive search, Rebecca appeared and calmly declared, "I'm not quite ready. I haven't found myself yet!" We all laughed. Rebecca and my brother actually made it to the semifinal match. Toward the end of the quarter-final game, Rebecca had to score a hole in one to keep her team in the game. Everyone watched in excitement and awe as Rebecca's last toss hit the board and somehow crawled over other bags and dropped in the hole. It was the "toss of the tournament"!

Another memorable moment occurred in the kitchen. My family has strong Italian, Brooklyn roots, and cooking good food has always been important. The kitchen is a place we all like to hang out, smell the wonderful aromas, and make sure the taste is up to our standards.

Rebecca Reflects:

We were all hanging out in the kitchen when all of a sudden, I felt compelled to loudly share: "I have an announcement to make. I love Stephen! He is amazing!"

Everyone was silent except for Stephen's brother.

With raised eyebrows, he retorted, "Rebecca, settle down. I have some stories for you about Stephen that are *not* so amazing!"

Stephen Reflects:

Wiffle ball is another family tradition. Its roots go all the way back to my childhood. Actually it goes back generationally, when my father, as a young boy growing up in Brooklyn, used to play stickball with other local boys. Every year at Lobster Fest, my father, my brother, and I play our annual Whiffle ball tournament. The winner has bragging rights for the year. The competition was lively in 2010, as we were all evenly matched. The highlight for my brother and me was seeing our "Pops" play his heart out, like he was twelve years old on the streets of Brooklyn. He was the one who was diving for balls all over the field. One year, he flung himself into the bushes for a ball and broke his toe on a concrete paver. Watching him pitch was a sight to behold as he imitated legends like Luis Tiant, Fernando Valenzuela, and others. My brother, two of the grandchildren, and I watched in awe and laughter as he delivered each pitch.

We are all extremely competitive, so it doesn't take long for an argument to break out about some rule or issue that inevitably arises. My brother tends to make up rules that favor him in the moment. We were in the middle of the tournament, and my brother was leading both Pops and me by a few runs late in the game. I began ripping hits off my brother. In the middle of this, David paused and announced, "By this time next year, Stephen may be married!" There was a sacred silence that hovered over the field of play for a few moments. We then resumed play, and I wound up winning the tournament. I was crowned the 2010 Wiffle Ball Champion! This fact is something I let Pops and my brother know throughout the year—so much so, they were dying to get a piece of me in 2011.

The next part of our courtship involved meeting Rebecca's mom and younger brothers who lived in Southern California. At this time we also wanted Rebecca to meet my mom, who lived in Pennsylvania. Since we did not have the funds to make two trips, Rebecca suggested that we invite my mom to California as well.

En route to Southern California, I received this message from my Pops: "Great travels. Fun time. Be yourself; love to Rebecca from the crazy Anthony clan." I arrived in the Long Beach airport with red roses in my hand and homemade chocolate chip cookies for the women in my life. I had recently started selling these cookies in a local ice-cream shop. It had been a dream of mine to start a business making my mom's chocolate chip cookies. She was an amazing baker and a renowned cook among our friends. We literally had two friends sneak into our house when we were away and steal chocolate chip cookies from the freezer, where my mom always kept a stash. Thus, in the summer of 2010, Momma Anthony's Classic Chocolate Chip Cookie was born.

It was a fun and exciting weekend. Some of the highlights for me, beside being with Rebecca and meeting her family, were my first experience of In-N-Out Burger (fantastic), surfing with Rebecca's brothers, and enjoying the weather and views of Long Beach.

We spent one day surfing at the beach. After about three hours bonding in the water with Rebecca's brothers, they had some beach games they wanted to "test" me with. It appeared that her brothers wanted to show me that their family was competitive as well. I am sure they had heard all about the intense games at Lobster Fest from Rebecca. It was clear that they didn't want the Anthonys to show up the Fullers. I was on their turf now! So, we played paddleball and bocce ball until I was tired out and just wanted to enjoy the calming rhythms of the waves (yes, I just wanted to take a nap on the beach).

It was another wonderful weekend with Rebecca. Now that the families had met, I excitedly set my sights toward the proposal!

Rebecca Reflects:

I was touched by how our moms immediately connected and enjoyed each other's company. We loved seeing them rejoice together over their answered prayers. I also enjoyed seeing Stephen and my brothers bond over surfing. I wasn't surprised that my mom, brothers, Grandma, and best friends all thoroughly enjoyed meeting Stephen. It was a treat to finally introduce everyone to the man I loved and wanted to spend the rest of my life with.

For Reflection:

1. How would you describe your family get-togethers?
2. If you have in-laws, or desire to have future in-laws, take a moment to ask God to lead you in a prayer of blessing over them.

CHAPTER 9

He is all I've ever hoped for, for you!

Rebecca Reflects:

We were delighted that our long-distance relationship encouraged us to exchange many snail-mail letters, cards, and e-mails. Receiving words of affirmation is one of the primary ways that I feel loved, and these letters were precious items that will be keepsakes forever. Here are a few excerpts from our love letters to each other.

> *June 2010: Rebecca Dawn Fuller, **I love you!** I never imagined I could feel this way about a woman, but you have literally captured my heart. I feel "undone" by you. My heart is overflowing with gratitude to God this morning for His gift to me—you! Thank you for waiting for me all these years!*
>
> *August 2010: Stephen, I have missed you **a lot** this weekend! I am looking forward to dancing with you through life. . . .*

> *December 2010: I love you, Stephen! And my love for you is being strengthened day by day. I couldn't be more grateful for God's kindness in bringing us together. You have made me one happy woman, just by being you, and by your choosing to love me. Thank you for wanting me to be your bride. May you always know how much I respect you and believe in you.*

> *May 2010: Stephen, every day I find myself smiling, wanting to celebrate the fact that I now know you and that I get to date you. Discovering details about who you are and moving forward with you toward marriage is so good and right. I continue to feel God's joy supporting us. Each day, out of God's goodness, our connection is only deepening. It's amazing to feel so free to be myself with you. Thank you for accepting me. I hope you always feel freedom to be yourself with me.*

To conclude, here are a few words of confirmation from some of my (Rebecca's) best friends:

> *So THRILLED for this exciting season in your life. Every part of this relationship seems so God-breathed, refreshing and like YOU . . . couldn't imagine it all happening any other way!*

He's adorable! All I've ever hoped for you!

Love him! And couldn't stop taking in the two of you together. Sigh. My heart is happy.

After being married for over six years (six years!), I still think the discovery of love is the most mysterious and amazing thing ever. It is constant, yet the beginning is so incredibly precious and unique. You sound like you are floating, dancing, singing with joy and wonder. It is beautiful. I only wish I could be there to see it for myself!

I am really excited for your life and for what God is doing. I am so proud of you, sister. I think Stephen and you are great for each other. You will grow so much having such a good man in your life. He is blessed to have you.

For Reflection:

1. We believe the Holy Scriptures are God's love letter to us. One of our favorite examples comes from Zephaniah 3:17: "The Lord your God is with you, the Mighty Warrior who saves. He will take great delight in you; in his love he will no longer rebuke you, but will rejoice over you with singing." Let God speak words of life and truth over you.

2. Who are the life-giving and supportive people in your world right now? How might God be inviting you to reach out to them as you pursue your deepest longings and dreams?
3. If you are dating or are engaged, what have your most trusted friends and family said to you about your relationship?

CHAPTER 10

It doesn't matter what you like; it's about what she likes!

Stephen Reflects:

Marriage proposals typically involve a token of commitment—the engagement ring. Early on, I had told Rebecca that the way we did things back on the East Coast, where I'm from, was the man got the ring and the woman either liked it or pretended to like it. Well, Rebecca said that the way they did things on the West Coast was the woman picks out the ring and the man buys the ring and presents it to the woman. Let the games begin.

Rebecca Reflects:

Most of my friends agreed that our input matters, since this is something we will wear for the rest of our lives. Early on, and in a bit of a panic, I emphatically told Stephen, "I don't even know what type of ring I would like, so how will you know?" Stephen seemed disappointed that I didn't want to be completely surprised, but he was open to hearing my feedback. Thus, we began the ring shopping adventure, together.

We came across many lovely rings, but I became overwhelmed with how outrageously expensive everything seemed. Plus, it was difficult for me to imagine enjoying a specific style for life. In high school I loved wearing colorful vintage-style clothes from the 60s and 70s and *big* hooped earrings; then in college I went through a stage where I loved sunflowers and often wore necklaces and T-shirts displaying the bright flower. Those tastes are now distant memories. Since my style has changed drastically over the years, I didn't know how I was going to pick something that I would like through the decades. I also felt pressured to find something quickly so that we could get engaged.

At one point, I felt completely stuck and in need of a shopping break. I gave Stephen a list of the things I wanted in a ring, and the plan was for him to take things from there.

Stephen Reflects:

Shortly after Rebecca's self-imposed ring-shopping break, I found "the one." I sent Rebecca a picture and announced to some of my guy friends that I had found an amazing ring that *I* liked. One of my friends quickly responded, "Stephen, it doesn't matter what *you* like; it's about what *she* likes!" The other friends who heard nodded, knowingly.

Well, Rebecca didn't quite like the ring, saying it was too masculine. I guess that is why I liked it!

Rebecca Reflects:

I'm grateful that I could be completely honest with Stephen. Seeing the ring he had initially picked out helped me realize that I wanted something more delicate and feminine. The search continued. Everything I tried on was beautiful, but I couldn't decide what style best suited *me*. I hoped to have a magical moment where I would spontaneously hug the jeweler, while exclaiming, "I love it! This is it!" So far, that hadn't happened.

Stephen Reflects:

My visit to propose to Rebecca was fast approaching. I had run out of time to find a ring that Rebecca loved. Little did she know I had a plan B.

CHAPTER 11

Yes!

Stephen Reflects:

I had no idea how exciting it would be to plan a romantic and memorable marriage proposal to the woman I love. I had witnessed many friends plan and prepare to ask the big question of their potential future bride. I had often wondered if I would ever get the chance to experience this for myself.

Later in September, on my way back to Grand Junction after asking Rebecca's father for permission to marry his daughter, I spent a night car camping near the base of Mt. Sherman, a 14,000-foot mountain. The next day I climbed this mountain. I have always enjoyed climbing mountains. It felt really good to spend some alone time seeking God and experiencing the beauty and challenge of climbing. As I hiked, a passage from the Bible came to mind that is a life verse to me. "For the eyes of the Lord range throughout the earth to strengthen those whose hearts are fully committed to him." (2 Chronicles 16:9). I sensed God's continued confirmation and joy about uniting me with Rebecca in marriage. I also spent some time thinking through how I wanted the proposal to go. Thus, on October 7, 2010, I flew to Seattle to ask my Love to marry me. She was the woman I had waited for and was clearly the gift God had for me.

Rebecca Reflects:

I was convinced that Stephen wouldn't propose the weekend he came to visit in October. He was adamant that he wanted to have the ring before asking me to marry him. Unfortunately, we hadn't been able to find the right ring yet.

The Thursday afternoon of Stephen's arrival, as I said good-bye to my last client, we both noticed a dozen red roses propped up against my office door. I was completely taken by surprise. Before Stephen came along, I never got flowers from guys, let alone gorgeous red roses. As I stood straining my neck to catch a glimpse of a hiding, grinning Stephen, I barely heard my client as she smiled enthusiastically and said, "Bye. Have a *great* weekend!"

Stephen was nowhere to be found. As I picked up the roses, I noticed a card on the floor by the door. Stephen had written, "I'm here! Come to me! You'll find me at your apartment. (Don't go to the airport!) Love, Your Boyfriend." I felt too excited and nervous to go straight home. I needed a few minutes to collect myself. So I decided to go get a manicure, like originally planned. My fingernails desperately needed some pampering, and it gave me a chance to catch my breath. Maybe, subconsciously, I knew my nails needed to look their very best that weekend.

As my apartment complex came into view, I was immediately intrigued by the mango-colored Camero that was parked a few yards away from the entrance to my apartment. I approached my front door, full of curiosity and eager anticipation. Before me was another note. "Look for me near the orange car. I love you!" First things first. I made a dash for my bathroom, retouched up my hair and makeup, and exchanged my work clothes for a more stylish outfit. After perhaps twenty minutes, I was finally ready to go to my Love. As I tentatively approached the mango sports car, I almost missed seeing Stephen. He had the front seat in a reclined position. He had apparently dozed off. I wondered how long I had made him wait!

It was wonderful to be embraced in a warm hug by my handsome boyfriend. Stephen suggested I change into warmer clothes before we went out for the evening. It ended up taking awhile to get out the door, as somehow I lost my cell phone and keys on the way out. I was running around in circles, flustered and giddy, and Stephen was patient as always.

Stephen blindfolded me with one of my colorful scarves, and off we went on our adventure. I had absolutely no clue where we were headed. When he took off my blindfold, I was standing in one of my favorite places, the entrance to the indoor labyrinth at St. Mark's Cathedral in Seattle. This is a place where I have had many meaningful experiences with God. The summer I finished graduate school, my dad, stepmom, and I had a significant and encouraging prayer time there regarding my future husband. I left that prayer time convinced that God had not forgotten me, and that He was preparing my heart to meet an amazing man. Also, for the past four New Year's Eves, I walked this guided meditation as a way to let go of the past year and embrace all God had for me in the new year. Additionally, as Stephen previously mentioned, he and I had already visited this labyrinth together. It was important for me to be with a man who was open to contemplative and prayerful spiritual practices such as walking a labyrinth.

Even after all the buildup, I still did not think a proposal was on the horizon. When Stephen got down on one knee, I felt so wobbly and full of emotion that I felt the need to get down on one knee too. Somehow, I remained standing. Stephen went on to passionately share from the depths of his heart. He said, "Rebecca, I love you! I want to protect you, provide for you, advance God's kingdom with you, make love to you, and raise children with you. I believe you are God's gift to me. Would you do me the honor of being my wife?"

I immediately yelled, "YES!" Even if the church hadn't been empty, I still would have yelled my answer. I wanted the whole wide world to know that Stephen Francis Anthony had asked me, Rebecca Dawn Fuller, to be his bride! It was the best thing that had ever happened to me.

Then Stephen kissed me. It was our first kiss, full of tenderness and the sweet promise of more to come. Stephen surprised me again by presenting me with a gorgeous diamond platinum ring. I was speechless. I couldn't stop staring and was amazed at how beautiful it was. My heart was bursting with joy, and I felt so energized that I started running and dancing in circles around the labyrinth maze.

Stephen Reflects:

Now that you know that the proposal happened, here is some background:

I had a lot of joy as I began planning the proposal. I had lots of ideas, and the centerpiece was asking Rebecca "the question" on a boat. A few weeks before the planned trip to Seattle, I made a jaunt over the beautiful Rocky Mountains to Colorado Springs to meet with Rebecca's dad and stepmom. I had initially planned to meet with just her father to ask for permission to marry his daughter. Her stepmom, knowing what I was up to, asked to come along as well, and I am glad she did. Not knowing the area, I had them pick their favorite restaurant. They had both played a significant role in our relationship, in bringing us together and providing wise insights for us. I was grateful for the opportunity to thank them with a delicious meal. It was a lot of fun reminiscing about the weekend Rebecca and I met. While we had a wonderful time, I was hesitant at first to share my plans regarding the proposal. Finally, I shared that I wanted to propose to Rebecca on a boat, but I wasn't quite sure if that was the best spot. Her stepmom spoke up and said, "Oh, I think St. Mark's Cathedral would be the ideal place for Rebecca." As soon as she said this, I exclaimed, "Yes! You're right; that is the best place!"

Rebecca Reflects:

After the proposal in St. Mark's Cathedral, I was yet again surprised when Stephen announced, "The night is young, and we have more celebrating to do." About twenty minutes later, we arrived at our next destination, and he guided me out of the convertible. I immediately smelled salty sea air. When he removed my blindfold, seagulls were soaring effortlessly in a blue sky with puffy white clouds, and sailboats were lounging in the dock. We were standing in a Seattle Marina near Golden Gardens, a favorite spot of mine.

As we walked toward the boats, a friend from graduate school greeted us. It appeared that Stephen knew him too. Stephen could tell I was confused, and with a big grin on his face he filled me in: "I've rented Greg's sailboat for the evening."

Wow! I was thrilled. I had never been sailing before. The captain and his mates seemed pleased at the happy news of our engagement. We dined at a little table on the top deck, where we were served red wine and a wonderful meal that Stephen had arranged to be catered in. The meal included a delicious bruschetta tomato appetizer, followed by perfectly seasoned salmon with grilled vegetables, orzo, and a molten lava melt-in-your-mouth chocolate cake. It all tasted divine.

We then set sail on what turned out to be a perfect Seattle night—crisp, clean air, stormy waters, and an interesting sky that showcased changing shades of blue and grey with hints of yellow. Thankfully, there was no rain. The captain and his crew were thoughtfully attentive, making sure our hot chocolates were always topped off and the music was to our liking. But they also gave us plenty of privacy. I especially loved being silly and reenacting some Titanic moments at the front of the sailboat. We were splashed with sea breeze as I spread out my arms and leaned into the safety of my handsome fiancé.

Stephen had the opportunity to sail the boat and proved to be quite adept. He confidently sailed us back to the marina. I too had attempted steering the boat. This only lasted about twenty seconds before we all realized that this was not such a good idea. I will be forever grateful to Stephen for giving us such a memorable and romantic adventure!

It was a magically memorable night, and we sealed it with passionate kissing on a private corner of one of the piers. Kissing Stephen was, yet again, another thing that had been well worth the wait!

For Reflection:

1. Write about your pursuit of someone's heart. Or, write about when you felt pursued by someone. Take time to give God any current desires you may have to be pursued and romanced.
2. Reflect on a time you experienced Jesus pursuing and loving your heart. If you have never had such an intimate experience, and would like to have one, share your desires with God.
3. If you're married, let your spouse know your favorite moment(s) of your proposal story.

CHAPTER 12

It's a reminder of God's faithfulness.

Stephen Reflects:

Two months before I proposed to Rebecca, when I was visiting her in Seattle, I received a phone message from my mom. Her voice sounded excited and reverent as she asked that I call her back immediately. Here is the ring story in her own words:

> *God hears and answers our prayers. Do we really believe that? God's Word tells us to be persistent in our prayers. So after many years of praying by many people, on April 24th, the Lord answered a very special prayer. The Lord arranged for Stephen and Rebecca to meet. On April 27th, Stephen called to tell me that he met the girl that he is going to marry. These words I thought would never come from my son's lips, but I knew, without a doubt, that this was the answer to my persistent prayers.*

On May 15th, three weeks after Stephen and Rebecca met, and after my trip to visit Stephen in Colorado, I went to visit some new friends who lived a few blocks away. I was not about to tell many people how the Lord had answered our prayers because I felt that the story was very sacred and many people would not understand. Upon entering their apartment, the husband began asking me about my trip to Colorado. He asked about my son, whom he had never met, and he continued in conversation about how difficult it was to meet a spouse in Colorado and offered suggestions on available options. This subject was never brought up by me. I continued to offer surface answers and just did not want to go into any conversation about my son, his singleness, or anything else concerning him. But he was politely persistent in this area, and finally I mentioned that Stephen had met someone three weeks earlier, and I began to tell the story of how the Lord had orchestrated the whole weekend of April 24th. His wife was also present in the room, and her only comment was "I have the goose bumps."

Then the wife got out of her chair and went into the bedroom. She returned with a small, dark blue velvet box and told me that she had been asking the Lord to give her direction in knowing whom she should give this diamond ring to, a ring that she had received from a godly Christian woman fifteen years earlier. But God knew long before who was going to receive this ring. I then opened the velvet box to find a beautiful diamond ring with a platinum setting. I was speechless and did not know why someone would be giving me this ring for my son, whom she never met. But God knew. My mind raced as to why I could not accept such a gift, but all I could think of was something that Rebecca had told Stephen the first day that she met him: "Stephen, I hear that the Lord wants to shower down His love on you." The other thought that raced through my mind was "Susan, don't interfere with the work and plans of God." Oh, by the way, the wife also produced the appraisal of the ring that she had received fifteen years earlier. I was shocked to see the quality and value of the ring, but the thought in my head was that God only gives us the best. I also felt that the ring was God's confirmation of Stephen and Rebecca's relationship. It will be a testimony for years to come of God's desire to have an intimate relationship with each of us. I

> *feel so humbled to be part of God's plan in my son's life and in Rebecca's life. Every time I tell this story to someone, I feel a sense of awe as they see God's love and grace.*

Wild story, huh? This story was another confirmation that God was the Author of our love story. It provided great comfort and security because of my fears of divorce and my uncertainties about choosing a mate. Growing up in a divorced home created much difficulty and emotional pain. I believe that one of the reasons I went into the counseling profession was to seek more healing for myself. Also, marriage was an intimidating proposition because I had this history of divorce in my family, and I wanted to make sure I made a wise choice. Obviously, there were many women out there, and I seriously questioned God after my previous relationship had failed. On paper, it had appeared we were a fantastic match. But even after relocating to live near her, this relationship ended with heartbreak for both of us. Thus, I asked God, "There are so many wonderful women out there; how do I know who is the right one to marry?"

When I was in Denver, I had a mentor who was working in a Christian youth ministry. One of the young people in this ministry was a teenage girl whose mother was single due to a divorce. My mentor heard God speak to him about this young girl's mother even before he met her. The message was "She is going to be your wife!" I remember being a bit jealous of him because of this, wanting God to speak to me as well. I also used to think about Adam in the Bible, and how easy it was for him. God brought the woman to him and said, "Here you go. Enjoy!" There was no such thing as eHarmony or Match.com, dating, courting, or seeing if they were compatible. It was a breeze for him! Why wouldn't God do this for me?

Therefore, as the events of meeting Rebecca unfolded, I was deeply humbled and in awe of the work of God in our lives to bring us together. God also had amazingly provided this ring for Rebecca. Even though I already knew in my heart that I wanted to marry her, I took this as another confirmation of God's blessing on our relationship.

Another thing that was fantastic about the proposal was that Rebecca had no idea that I was going to propose to her that particular weekend. She didn't think I had the engagement ring yet, and I had told her that I would not propose without a ring. I had kept the whole ring story to myself.

The ring was a diamond set in a traditional setting. Rebecca said she liked antique-style rings. I figured that I could always have a jeweler move the diamond to a new setting that Rebecca liked. After prayer and consultation with friends, I decided to give Rebecca the ring and let her choose what she wanted to do with it. It turned out she *loved* the ring and the story of how the ring had come to us.

Rebecca Reflects:

It was a gorgeous ring. Even more special than the ring's brilliance and charm was the amazing story of God surprising us with such an extravagant gift. I decided I didn't want to change a thing.

We were amazed at how God used the generosity of two strangers in Pennsylvania to encourage and bless us in such a mighty way. I was grateful that the woman who gave us the ring waited on God to lead her. Also, I was amazed at how Christ used Stephen's mom, and each of our parents, to be intricately involved in our love story.

The ring was above and beyond anything I could have hoped for! No wonder I couldn't find another ring. Every time I look at my ring, I am reminded of God's generous love and provision. I can only imagine the sheer delight it brought God to orchestrate such a miraculous surprise.

For Reflection:

1. What gifts have brought you the most joy?
2. Reflect on gifts you've enjoyed giving out over the years.

CHAPTER 13

I'd rather move to the desert if God is inviting me there, than live in lush meadows of my own choosing

Stephen Reflects:

Rebecca and I began our engagement with much excitement. I suppose this is how most, if not all, engaged couples begin. The big looming question for us became *who would have to move?*

Rebecca Reflects:

I first moved to Seattle as a graduate student, and the overcast rainy days were the perfect backdrop to cozying up with my counseling books and a cup of hot chocolate at Zoco's coffee shop. It was less tempting to ditch my studies and go swimming, or hiking, when the weather was damp and drizzly. By my seventh year living there, the constant stream of overcast days, often even in summer months, was starting to bother me. Nonetheless, even with the lack of sunshine, Seattle was still my dream city. It had lush evergreen trees, magnificent mountain views, numerous crisp and clean lakes, and a thriving dance and music scene. Most importantly I felt deeply connected to my friends there. Even though I still wanted to lay down permanent roots in Seattle, I did admit to Stephen that Seattle was starting to lose its luster and charm because he wasn't there.

Stephen and I both began to seek the Lord's guidance as to what He had for us. At one point, Stephen even had close friends pray with him. He wanted to be more open to the possibility of moving. I appreciate that Stephen didn't just assume that because I was the woman, and because he had his own business and house, I would be the one who would need to move.

As I do with most big decisions, I began with writing out a pro and con list. I felt confident that my reasons for staying in Seattle would far outweigh my reasons for moving to Colorado. After a few days, my list felt done. I asked the Lord to open my eyes to what He wanted me to notice as I read through each point. I was shocked at how many positive things I had listed about moving to Colorado. For example, if I moved to Colorado, I would be closer to my dad and stepmom. I would also have more opportunities to go hiking, fishing, and camping, activities I have thoroughly enjoyed the few times I have done them. As I reviewed my lists, God began to open my eyes to the fact that Colorado was clearly where Stephen was meant to be, at least for now. As I prayed, I sensed that new friendships awaited, as well as unique opportunities to partner with my husband and live into the vocational mission that God had for us.

Over the next few months, God continued to speak to me about moving. One day, as I was praying on a park bench, I gazed in awe at the gloriously breathtaking Olympic Mountains that framed the Puget Sound. Jesus reminded me that Seattle was not the only beautiful place He had created. He assured my heart that I would find and experience beauty again in other places. Also, many friends, even Seattle friends who adamantly did not want to see me move, began to share how they too could envision me happily making my home in Colorado. Months later, during a time of listening prayer, a dear friend and I began to hear God inviting me to "move to Stephen." God was clearly inviting me to a person, Stephen, more than He was inviting me to a place, Colorado.

The final confirmation came during a benediction given by a pastor at my Seattle church. My pastor looked straight at me and said, "I'd rather move to the desert if God is inviting me there, than live in green and lush meadows of my own choosing." Stephen lived in a high mountain desert town. I left that church service knowing deep within my soul that the God of the universe was giving me the peace my heart needed to take the next step. That evening, I let Stephen know that I felt God was inviting me to move to him. Here is what Stephen later wrote me regarding my moving.

> *December 2010: Rebecca, as I went hiking yesterday, I was thinking of you (I think about **You** a lot these days!). I was reflecting on how much you are sacrificing and leaving behind: wonderful and numerous friends, a thriving and rewarding counseling practice that you have poured yourself into, the beauty of Seattle, music venues and cultural events, and many memories.*
>
> *Rebecca, I just want to say, "**Thank you!**" Thank you for being willing to go wherever God leads you. Just know that I am waiting for you here in Colorado with joyful anticipation and excitement! All that I have is yours as well! I look forward to living life with you, being one with you in body, mind, soul, and spirit—"the two shall become one."*

Stephen understood how much I had loved Seattle, and I felt cared for after hearing him acknowledge all that I would be leaving.

Stephen Reflects:

All along, I sensed that Colorado was the right place for us. But, I waited and prayed that God would speak directly to Rebecca rather than share this with her. I knew that Rebecca loved God and listened to Him. I also believed she would take the news better from Him than from me. I did not want her to resent me. If it came from God, she would have to wrestle with Him. It was encouraging to hear Rebecca say, "Seattle is losing its luster and charm because it is missing you." It was also encouraging to hear the other specific ways God was leading Rebecca to me. I remember thinking to myself, *Yes, thank you, Father, for clearly leading both of us.*

Rebecca Reflects:

I'm thankful my roommate suggested that I move to Colorado to live near Stephen before our wedding. It gave us time to discover even more about each other. We went on weekly dates: hiking, ballroom dancing, and attending plays and dance performances at the local college. It also gave me space to get to know Colorado a bit on my own. I love exploring a new city's downtown area, coffee shops, restaurants, and parks. Plus, it gave us time to prepare Stephen's house for my arrival. Stephen keeps an orderly and neat house, but it did need my special touch, and I spent time deep cleaning and organizing. I also had time to work on wedding details, such as finding a local wedding photographer, planning the décor for our wedding reception, and finding a place to buy our flowers. It was all much easier to do in person.

Stephen Reflects:

On my end, I was thrilled about the upcoming wedding, but I also had my hands full. My counseling practice was only six months old and needed constant nurturing. When I didn't have clients, I would introduce myself to those who worked in my building. And, I would take pastors out to lunch to learn more about their ministries and let them know that I'd love to be a resource for their church. I wanted to provide valuable and quality help to my existing clients while simultaneously building the practice. I also had committed to host and mentor a young man with learning disabilities who had grown up in a broken home without ever knowing his father. On top of this, I had started a basement remodeling project. Needless to say, I was quite busy.

In November, I attended a six-day experiential leadership seminar in San Francisco (through a leadership organization called Klemmer). I was encouraged to continue to not settle for less than the best in life. One of the goals I set while at this event was to write a book, which you are now reading. Writing a book had been on my heart for the past several years. I believe each person has a story to tell.

For Reflection:

1. Have you ever been asked to let go of something or someone you deeply loved? If so, take time to write about the emotions that this experience brought up for you.
2. Think about a time in your life when you made a big decision. Journal about what the decision-making process looked like for you (how did you arrive at your decision?).
3. Is there a decision you are in the midst of right now? Take time to ask for and receive God's wisdom and guidance.

CHAPTER 14

I want to make out with him 24-7

Rebecca Reflects:

The first nine months of our dating relationship was long distance, which made it easier to stay sexually pure. Actually, what helped even more than not being able to physically reach out and touch each other was Stephen's belief that it was best not to start kissing until we got engaged. At first, I was not thrilled with this prospect, and I tried to change Stephen's mind on numerous occasions. But, he was convicted that this was the best decision *for us*. It would have been easy to push the envelope if we had been kissing all along, because when we did visit each other, we were both full of intense passion and excitement. This boundary helped us immensely to not take things too far.

Once we got engaged, kissing was great fun, but with it came more passion and an increased desire for more, thus making it much more challenging to stay sexually pure.

The following are entries I wrote in my journal:

March 11, 2011: God, I wanted to check in with You about my physical relationship with Stephen. He and I sense You inviting us to not lie down on top of each other. Even though we're fully clothed, when we do lie down together, our make-out times become extra passionate. You are clearly speaking, but our actions show that we would rather do what feels good rather than listen to Your voice. Why do I continue to think I know what's best?

Tonight, we repented to the Lord and to each other, asking for forgiveness. Thank you, God, for your grace, mercy, and forgiveness. I want to trust that You do have our best interest in mind. I know we need to be cautious, but at the same time I am grateful that our connection and desire for each other is so strong.

March 12, 2011: Being with Stephen tonight was full of fun and ease. But we seemed greedy with each other regarding the ways we interacted physically. God, I hear You saying that Stephen and I need to be patient and wait for Your perfect timing. You want to bless us with rich and passionate intimacy, but it's not ours to partake of just yet. Soon physical intimacy will be Your beautiful gift to us. Jesus, please empower me to receive Your words and Your instructions. Lord, You are reminding me that the marriage bed is to be kept pure, even in these final days of our engagement.

Lord, You know how hard it is for us, and for many couples, to stop making out when it gets extra hot and heavy. Thus, I wonder if it's like You're saying, "Stay clear of going down that road." I clearly sense that if we continue with such steamy make-out times on Stephen's bed, we'll enter marriage with shame and regret, and I know that You don't want that for us. I want more for us too. Thank you for speaking to me, Lord.

March 22, 2011: Lord, I am so hungry for Stephen's loving touches, and I can't wait to be united with him in every way. I just want to make out with him 24-7, and he seems to not be able to get enough of me either! Being full of passion and desire is good, the way God created me to be. But also, self-control is a fruit of the Spirit that right now I don't see in my life. Yet again, even though it's great fun, we know that choosing to stay away from times on Stephen's bed helps us to not have regrets.

March 25, 2011: Today I sense God saying that it'll be even more fun lying down on our marriage bed if we stop lying down now. Lord, please show me how to be affectionate while still being full of self-control and respect for Stephen's body, as well as my own body. Ultimately You, God, not Stephen, or anyone else, can satisfy the deepest longings of my heart. Lord, I hear You inviting me to bring You my deep hunger and thirst.

Stephen Reflects:

For me, not kissing until we were engaged was a huge help to stem the tide of passion. Also, while we were dating, Rebecca heard stories of numerous women who had premarital sex during their dating and engagement periods. These women confessed to Rebecca their sadness about this and their loss of respect for their husbands. They felt that their men did not stand up and protect them by establishing and keeping healthy boundaries. For many of them, it was a breach of trust, and it did not set up a solid footing for their marital relationship. All this was a reminder and warning to me of the importance of fighting for purity in my relationship with Rebecca.

Most of all, I knew that God was clear about when and where to have sex. My love and respect for God, for Rebecca, and for myself kept me from taking what was not mine to enjoy yet. Also, it helped that in my previous dating relationships I had not been very physical. For example, I didn't kiss every woman that I had dated. Because I hadn't gone down certain sexual roads, I was content kissing Rebecca, without pressing her to go further than this. While my desire for Rebecca was strong, I'm grateful that God enabled me to have self-control. I knew from experience that walking with God and following His plan for life was the wisest decision.

Rebecca Reflects:

God was specific with us regarding the topics of making out while lying down and lying down on top of each other. Other than this, God didn't have us focus on what we couldn't or shouldn't do together physically. Instead, God invited us to follow His ways so we could receive all the joy and fulfillment for which we were created. We were prompted to focus on the life-giving things that God *was* lovingly inviting us to do. As a result, we enjoyed the simple and sweet forms of affection that can easily be forgotten in dating relationships. We enjoyed activities that brought joy and closeness, like giving each other love letters, hand holding, candlelit romantic dinners, hugging, and hand and foot caresses.

We were thankful for God's empowerment to remain virgins. We did not stay sexually pure because we were righteous or self-disciplined. It was only by the Lord's grace, mercy, and clear loving guidance that we did not give away the gift of our virginity. We praise God for the ways He reminded us of the true and lasting intimacy that awaited us in marriage, and for the ways He clearly guided us through this exciting and sexually tempting time.

For Reflection:

1. If you are in a romantic relationship, ask God what He wants to say to you about your physical relationship.
2. What are the physical and affectionate acts that God is inviting you to partake in before marriage?
3. If you have had sex, we believe a soul tie has been formed between you and the person you were sexual with. We encourage you to meet with a trusted person in order to ask God to break the soul tie bond. If you have had any heartache from these experiences, know that Jesus loves you and wants to bring you freedom and healing.
4. Read through 1 Corinthians 6:12—20 in the Bible. These are verses that God has highlighted for us over the years. Ask God to speak to you regarding these truths.
   - *The body, however, is not meant for sexual immorality but for the Lord, and the Lord for the body (verse 13).*
   - *For it is said, "The two will become one flesh" (verse 16).*

- *Flee from sexual immorality. All other sins a person commits are outside the body, but whoever sins sexually, sins against their own body (verse 18).*
- *Do you not know that your bodies are temples of the Holy Spirit, who is in you, whom you have received from God? You are not your own; you were bought at a price. Therefore honor God with your bodies (verses 19 and 20).*

5. If you are married, ponder Song of Songs 5:1: "*Drink your fill of love.*" God is enthusiastic about us having intimacy and pleasure. Ask God to pour out His healing and joy in your marriage.

CHAPTER 15

How sweet it is to be loved by you

Stephen Reflects:

As soon as we were engaged, we began planning the wedding; we set the date for April 16. On the plane ride back from Seattle, I made a list of all of my family and friends who I wanted to be at this special event. I also began thinking about who I wanted to marry us. Two very influential men in my life came to mind, and I considered having both of them play a part. Finally, I settled on just one officiate. He and I met when I was sixteen years old at a Christian Sports Camp he started in central New Jersey. He has been a friend and mentor ever since. I have always admired his passion for Christ, love for people, vision, leadership style, and sense of humor. He has invested a lot in me through the years. When I asked him to marry us, he only asked that he be paid in Momma Anthony's Chocolate Chip Cookies.

We decided to get married in Colorado so that we would have the support of the local community at our wedding and in our marriage. Rebecca was still living in

Seattle, so it was up to me to explore venue options. We settled on getting married at First Presbyterian Church, where I was attending, and having our reception at La Puerta Dance Studio. I had been ballroom dancing at La Puerta for about a year, and they had recently moved into a beautifully restored ballroom on downtown Main Street. It was the perfect place to hold a wedding reception, and it turned out to be the first one that the owners of La Puerta had ever booked. I also went to work on choosing a caterer; let me tell you, this was hard work. Taste testing rich and decadent samples of bacon-wrapped scallops and jalapeño cream cheese crescent poppers from chefs seeking my business was a sacrifice, but someone had to do it. I think I gained a few pounds in the process, but I wasn't complaining.

With these tasks complete, I gladly left the rest of the planning in Rebecca's very capable hands. My father had cautioned me that sometimes the wedding planning takes on a life of its own. He had witnessed this with my two stepsisters. He wisely commented, "Stephen, every woman has thought about her wedding since she was a little girl. Just realize that this is *her* special day."

It was a joyful day when Rebecca landed at the airport in Colorado on January 9, 2011. Some friends of mine from church had graciously agreed to have Rebecca live with them, rent free, in the months leading up to the Big Day.

As counselors, both Rebecca and I were acutely aware of the importance of premarital counseling. We were eager to "practice what we preach" and go through this process for ourselves. We asked my pastor if he would be willing to guide us through the premarital work. It is critical to know as much information as possible so that one can make an educated decision regarding the question, "Do I really want to unite my life with this person?" Once this decision is made, it is also crucial for the husband to know what his wife's emotional wounds have been, the message of those wounds, and how she hides and shuts down when she feels overwhelmed and afraid so that he can fight for her.

Going into the premarital counseling process, I felt 100 percent certain that Rebecca was the one I wanted to marry and God's gift to me. I could see us partnering together with God to advance His work of loving and healing in this world. This was confirmed through the premarital sessions. Hearing Rebecca share her story with the pastor reminded me of the wounds she took on while growing up with a rage-filled father and experiencing the divorce of her parents. It was helpful to be aware of her deep hurts so that I could specifically fight for her and pray with her about any unworthiness issues and fears that might be lingering.

On top of this, we decided to take a thirteen-week course through Dave Ramsey's Financial Peace University. This nearly ended our engagement. Rebecca had a sizable amount of student loan debt from her undergraduate and graduate school studies. The hardest part for me was her denial of the issue. When I asked her how much she currently owed and how much her monthly payment was, her face turned ashen white and her eyes grew glossy and cold. Talking about finances seemed to be very triggering for Rebecca, and she would get silent and have a faraway look about her. As it turned out, she was ashamed that she was bringing such a huge amount of debt into the marriage. She was also embarrassed that she hadn't paid off more of her debt by now.

After one Financial Peace session, she said, "This course may have been super helpful, but right now I am so over Dave Ramsey!" She then suggested that we take a break so I could consider if I still wanted to marry her, debt and all! The amount of debt was disturbing to me and was difficult to swallow, I admit. However, I didn't need a break; I knew I still wanted to marry Rebecca.

After navigating all these obstacles, the Big Day finally arrived. Our family and friends descended upon Western Colorado to celebrate with us. Before the wedding, my brother and father had planned a three-day guys' getaway at a cabin located near the Colorado National Monument. It was a beautiful spot, a rustic mountain cabin overlooking a stunning canyon vista. It was a blast to have my closest friends there with me. I was also glad that they got to see and experience the grandeur of Western Colorado. I was secretly hoping that they would move their families near me, since Colorado is "God's Country." We enjoyed amazing food such as steaks, Italian Brooklyn sausages, homemade tomato sauce and pasta, cooked by my Italian father. We also played competitive games of Baggo, went for a rigorous hike in the Monument up Liberty Cap Trail, and enjoyed excellent conversation and male bonding. While I was reveling in this time, Rebecca was enjoying time with her nine bridesmaids. They had lots of fun and embarrassing things planned for her. They were glad to return to Rebecca some of the "medicine" she had dished out to them when they got married.

We had a large wedding party (eighteen total). Rebecca and I both were thankful for all the friends God had provided for us during our years of singleness. We wanted to honor them by having them stand with us at our wedding. Our ceremony turned out to be a wonderful time to celebrate God's faithfulness and goodness to us. The highlight was seeing Rebecca walk down the aisle. Her beauty took my breath away. This amazing, captivating woman was walking slowly and purposefully toward me, in front of our closest family and friends, with the sole purpose of uniting her life with mine. My heart overflowed with joy! This was the woman I had waited thirty-nine years for.

Another sacred moment included my tearing up during our vows, when I asked Rebecca to be my *wife*. It took me a few moments to regain my composure after I choked up with the thought of these words. Quite a few people started tearing up when they saw me crying. I was touched when I saw my big brother crying. Someone passed my father's handkerchief to me, which I used, and then I offered it to my brother. He laughed and refused, not wanting to come close to his brother's snot. Another highlight was having my cute nieces as the flower girls and my handsome nephew as the ring bearer. The ceremony was meaningful and honored God as the Giver of all good gifts.

After pictures with family at the front of the church, my brother had generously arranged for a limo ride for Rebecca and me to take us to a photo shoot, just the two of us. Later, one of my groomsmen announced our arrival at the reception. We danced a choreographed rendition of James Taylor's "How Sweet It Is"! It was magical to dance while being surrounded by our closest family and friends. It was a wonderful celebration of love and God's faithfulness!

During a premarital counseling session, our officiant asked us what we loved about each other. Unbeknownst to us, he recorded our answers and read them at our wedding ceremony! It ended up being a very special moment.

Stephen's words to Rebecca: "I love you, Rebecca! You are God's gift to me. When I first met you, I was so attracted to your beauty, and I was literally undone by your tenderness toward me. Everything about you is beautiful—your heart, your soul, your mind, and your outward beauty.

I love your body, your eyes, and your lips. I love kissing you. I just love being with you. I love dancing with you and hiking with you. I love the adventures we've already shared and those ahead. I love your walk with God. I love your passion. I'm excited about walking through life and serving the Lord with you."

Rebecca's words to Stephen: "From the second day we met and you prayed over our meal, I have loved you. I feel safe, loved, and protected by you. I love your heart. I love your passion. I love your strength and your tenderness. It's so rare to find a man who has both, and I prayed for that for a long time. I needed someone alive to God's grace, and you are. You help me to receive God's love and your love. I love how you love people—you really care. You're compassionate, not judgmental. You have beautiful humility, and I love how you fight for people. You're a good cook (but not as good as me). I love how sexy and hot you are. I can't wait to . . . I love your hair and your eyes. I love how you listen to God's voice and how you make me laugh. You will be a great father. I love to dance with you and worship God with you. You are such a gift to me."

Rebecca Reflects:

Our wedding weekend was magical. I finally got to marry my very best friend. I was fully present to the gifts of beauty and love all around me. I felt incredibly loved and more beautiful and alive than I had ever felt before. (The only thing that would have made the day better was if it had happened years earlier. We both desired marriage for years, before it finally came. Stephen says he didn't feel like he was ready sooner, though. I like to think that I was ready for marriage earlier in my life, but maybe I wasn't. After all, God did do a lot of significant healing in my life the final six months before meeting Stephen.)

The day before the wedding, I had a bridal luncheon where we savored curried chicken salad, homemade honey wheat rolls, fresh strawberries, and crisp white wine. After our meal, my best friends prayed prayers of thanksgiving over me. These faithful and loyal friends had for years and years eagerly awaited this day. They too rejoiced over the fact that Stephen was a man who walked intimately with Christ, who cherished my heart, and who daily showered me with God's love and gentle kindness. The afternoon was full of happy tears, hugs, knowing looks, and much laughing and rejoicing.

Our rehearsal dinner was a night of celebrating with delicious Caesar salad, lasagna, raspberry cheesecake, and thoughtful, funny, and kind toasts from our friends and family. My talented bridesmaids performed a song describing the story of how we met set to the tune of the song "Y.M.C.A." I can't resist sharing the lyrics, although the real joy was seeing them sing their hearts out with gusto! Glad we got it all on video!

Stephen, living in a small town
Looking, but there were no girls around
To Denver, to a conference he went
He got more than counseling insights

Rebecca was on a blind date
Her dad said, "But this Stephen guy's great"
Turns out, after all, Bill was right
Oh, those sparks they did fly

Chorus:
And Stephen said, "Come to GJ" (Becky held up a sign that said GJ)
Rebecca said, "Why not this way?" (Rachel held up a sign that said Seattle)
We all know who won, 'cause we're here for the fun
As this duo becomes one

Repeat Chorus
Meeting all your family and friends
Packing and selling all your loose ends
Surfing, competing at Lobster Fest
You both passed the big tests

Walking through a labyrinth of prayer
He popped the big question there
She said, you're my dream come true
I can't wait to marry you

Repeat Chorus
Look out GJ
Here come the Antho-nays
They'll make a great team as husband and wife
As together they'll dance through life.

The morning of our wedding, I awoke excited and well rested. Stephen and I had a simple breakfast and a sweet prayer time together. I am so glad we had scheduled this time to start our day together. Then I was off to the church to get dressed and ready.

My mom and I had gone wedding dress shopping together. We found a "wow" dress that I loved, and she ended up generously blessing us by buying it. The dress was ivory and strapless, with just enough beautifully placed diamond beading. The veil was long and romantic, and I wore it low. My shoes were sparkly silver. My earrings were dangling silver diamond jewels. My bracelet was a simple strip of diamonds. I felt gorgeous, like a princess. At the church, upbeat music was playing, yummy snacks were abundant, and I had professional stylists do my hair and makeup, a first for me. It was delightful to have such royal treatment.

Our wedding day turned out to be a warm and glorious seventy degrees. Every detail of our wedding was meaningful to us. We were forever grateful for all the ways our family, especially my mom, helped make our wedding dreams a reality. I loved the vibrant bouquets my mom designed and arranged. The flowers were gorgeous shades of raspberry/fuchsia and mango colors. She even added a few fuchsia feathers to my bridesmaids' bouquets. The colors "popped" against my bridesmaids' black dresses. My bridesmaids were extra grateful to me for letting them pick out their own black dresses. I wasn't worried, as they all have fantastic taste!

Before walking me down the aisle, my dad lovingly spoke words of blessing over me and my future husband. It was a gift to have my dad, a man full of God's grace, wisdom, and love, who had seen our love unfold from day one, walk me down the aisle toward my handsome groom. Other favorite moments included honoring each of our moms by giving them a single ivory rose, hearing the special music, inviting all our guests to partake in communion with us, and having our guests get out of their seats and lay hands on us while praying over us. After we passionately kissed, our loved ones blew bubbles at us as we joyfully ran up the aisle to Ray LaMontagne's song "You Are the Best Thing."

It was fun to then jump into an elegant white limousine and head to our own private photo shoot at a lovely house from the 1900s. This charming house had its own orchard full of white and pink blossoming trees, gorgeous aspens, and blooming flowers. It even had its own chicken coop.

Our reception site was a beautifully restored 102-year-old ballroom on Main Street. It's a favorite spot of ours for dancing on Friday nights. We entered the ballroom and immediately surprised everyone with a somewhat choreographed first dance. As we showed off our fun East Coast swing and Foxtrot dance moves, our guests were on their feet in a circle clapping, surrounding us with their cheers and loving support. Our first dance was definitely one of my very favorite moments. It's awesome to be married to a man who loves to dance as much as I do.

Our wedding was full of laughter, tears of joy, delicious red wine from California and Italy, loving toasts, and lots of fun and spirited dancing. Our guests again blew bubbles at us and sent us off with hugs and shouts of joy as we headed to a cozy bed-and-breakfast cottage nestled in nearby mountains for our first night together. I am grateful for all the friends and family that helped make it such an amazing and joy-filled day! It was truly the best day ever!

For Reflection:

1. If you could repeat a day, what day would you love to relive?
2. If you are married, describe some of your wedding highlights.
3. If you desire marriage, what are some words that you pray will describe your wedding day? What thoughts, ideas, and dreams do you have regarding your wedding day?

CHAPTER 16

Yeah baby, that's what I'm talking about

Stephen Reflects:

Driving to the bed-and-breakfast, our hearts incredibly full of love, I could hardly believe that I was about to share a bed with my beautiful bride. I began to imagine the bliss that awaited us. Suddenly I heard my new wife gasping for air. The lovely and tight-fitting wedding dress was squeezing the life out of her. Rebecca adjusted her seat so she could lay flat and breathe. She screamed, "Hurry up and get there so we can get this dress off me!"

"Yeah baby, that's what I am talking about," I proclaimed, as I hit the accelerator.

We pulled up to the bed-and-breakfast, and I excitedly carried my bride across the threshold of our room. We kissed passionately, and very carefully I untied Rebecca's wedding dress . . .

Rebecca Reflects:

It felt exhilarating having Stephen's strong and tender hands eagerly undress me and caress my inviting body. My body responded with delight and pleasure to his touch . . .

I would love to go on to share about how we had wild, passionate sex all night long. Sadly, however, that was not the case. Although our wedding night was full of sweet moments of connection, it was not all that I dreamed it would be.

Prior to our wedding, I discovered that I had many of the symptoms of a sexual disorder called vaginismus. *Vaginismus* may be a new word for you; it was for us. According to Mark and Lisa Carter, authors of *Completely Overcome Vaginismus*, "[It] is an involuntary contraction of the muscles surrounding the entrance to the vagina, making penetration impossible and/or painful."[5] According to vaginismus.com, it's commonly accepted that roughly two women in a thousand will experience vaginismus. The website says this number could be higher if more women would overcome embarrassment and seek help.

As I read their book, I learned that vaginismus was not due to lack of passion for one's mate, lack of trying to have sex, or any physical abnormality.

Some of the possible causes of vaginismus mentioned in the book that I resonated with were past sexual abuse, fear of pain, high anxiety, inadequate sex education, overly strict or unbalanced religious teaching in the home, exposure to shocking sexual imagery in childhood, parental fears, fear of commitment, and lack of trust. Other causes that I personally didn't resonate with include fear of pregnancy, painful intercourse as a result of a medical/physical condition, violence in the home, and having had an abusive partner.[6] I, like many vaginismus sufferers, had never been able to insert anything (such as a tampon or a gynecologist's exam tools) into my vagina.

Although it looked like I had vaginismus, I still hoped and prayed that the sexual passion Stephen and I had for each other would be enough to push past this condition. Sadly, even though we were full of love and desire for each other, when we did attempt to make love that first night, it was as if Stephen's body was hitting a wall, and intercourse was not possible. At long last, we had God's blessing to become one flesh, and we couldn't. We were both disappointed, but not completely shocked. I am grateful that, as hard as it was, I was completely honest with Stephen about my possible sexual condition before our honeymoon. We were both aware that intercourse would happen eventually, but most likely not right away.

Even though we didn't have intercourse our first night, I was extremely grateful for how comfortable Stephen and I were being intimate with each other. Since we had never spent the night together, there was a fresh newness and excitement to every unfolding moment. Thankfully, Stephen was able to figure out how to free me from what had become a highly constrictive and tight wedding dress. Shortly after, as Stephen happily undressed me from the playful, pink, polka-dot lingerie I had chosen, there was great joy and innocence. We praise God that we were free to be naked together for the first time, and there was no shame or embarrassment as we explored each other's bodies and discovered wonderful pleasure in each other's arms. I loved the wedding celebration, but I cherished these sacred moments where at last I was free to be alone with my handsome lover. In those moments, nothing else mattered but our intimate connection. Our bed was full of laughter, freedom, honest conversation, and unity. Even though I wasn't able to sleep a wink that first night (I've always had a hard time sleeping in new places), I still arose rested and in awe that I would now spend all my nights with this incredibly patient, compassionate, and sexy man.

In conclusion, our wedding night was bittersweet. Yes, there was joy in being together. But I also felt sad and disappointed that I was unable to open myself up and receive my husband in this intimate way. I felt like a failure, like I was the only woman in the world who couldn't properly perform sexually. Stephen had been so patient in waiting for us to have sex, and I wanted him to experience the bliss of oneness. I wanted the wait to be over for both of us.

The good news is that, according to Mark and Lisa Carter, vaginismus is 100 percent curable. "The treatment process involves retraining the mind and the body," they write. "The mind needs to be free of any negative inhibitions toward sex, for whatever reason, and the body needs to be retrained to accept vaginal penetration and pleasure."[7]

Stephen Reflects:

For me the wedding night was wonderful and disappointing. It was wonderful to undress my beautiful wife and explore and enjoy her naked, voluptuous body. It was frustrating as well, due to the fact that we were unable to have intercourse. This was not a shock, as both Rebecca and I were aware of the vaginismus, and knowing this helped to temper the disappointment. But, my silent prayer was "Really, God, here we both have waited to have sex because we love You and want to honor You, and now that we have Your blessing, we can't! God, how could You allow this to happen? We were faithful to You, and this is what we get. Thanks a lot!"

In his book *Disappointment With God*, author Philip Yancey addresses three questions that many people wonder about but seldom ask aloud: "Why is God unfair? Silent? Hidden?"[8] Both Rebecca and I were silently, and sometimes loudly, asking the first question, Is God unfair?

Rebecca (age thirty-five) and I (age thirty-nine), who were virgins when we married and had each intentionally saved ourselves for each other, were still waiting. I was celibate while single, and now I wondered if I would continue to be celibate even though I was now married.

For Reflection:

1. If you're married, describe your honeymoon. If you experienced disappointments or trauma, share your heart with God, and ask Him to speak to you and lead you into greater healing.
2. Take time to reflect on the following quote:

Christians encounter an oversexualized culture with an undersexualized spirituality. This distortion of purity depicts the good Christian as a disembodied spirit floating through this world on the way to heaven and portrays sex as something dangerous and dirty that ought to be kept in a darkened corner of life. Even when a person marries and sex suddenly becomes good and blessed, it is still kept in a corner. . . . This approach is an accident waiting to happen: what is repressed reappears, often in troubled form. Sex is a big deal and it deserves to be released from its darkened corner. [9]

3. Do you resonate with this quote? Why or why not?
4. If you are single, what words would you use to describe sex? If you are married, what are words you would use to describe your sex life?

CHAPTER 17

Nothing is impossible for Me

Stephen Reflects:

I heard a pastor say, "Marriage is God's sneaky way of getting a person crucified!" When you bring two imperfect people together, tension and friction are inevitable. Authors John and Staci Eldredge say that "marriage is fabulously hard."[10] For us, the first big battle we faced was vaginismus.

Rebecca Reflects:

During a prayer time with a dear friend, she shared that she believed that the Lord was going to use Stephen's loving presence as a major instrument to bring me healing in the area of my sexuality, specifically regarding my condition of vaginismus. While I was engulfed in shame, self-hatred, and despair, Stephen was kind and patient with me. He said he loved me, even if we could never have sex. It was reassuring to hear this, but I couldn't believe God would empower us to save ourselves for each other all this time to then have this be the end of the story. I had to believe there was more in store for us.

I wanted to be one with my husband, but I had been shut down as a woman for so long. Being a woman had not always felt good and safe. Witnessing some painful relationships my mom experienced with men convinced me to keep my walls up around them. And, living with my dad during formative years, when I started my menstrual cycle and began developing as a woman, was awkward, as he did not know how to help me through that difficult time. I began to ignore and downplay my femininity. For example, because I didn't want to make my dad uncomfortable with having to deal with a developing teenage daughter, I often wore my brothers' baggy clothes. Because of the relational heartache my mom faced, I tried not to attract male attention to myself. As I've alluded to earlier, anything my mom did, I decided not to do. She dated, so I didn't. She had gynecological exams, so I didn't. She wore makeup, even if she was just making a quick run to the grocery store. I only really put time into fixing my hair and makeup if it was a special occasion. Thus, I'm just now discovering things about my body and femininity I wished I'd learned years ago.

My prayer was that God would empower me and open me up to all the good gifts of freedom that He had for me as a woman. I knew this was a season of learning to have compassion and patience with myself. It was painful, and there were many tears. In my spirit, I felt ready to make love to Stephen and be one with him, but my mind and body were developmentally behind. I prayed that God's hope would wash over me.

What follows are some of my journal entries during this time of healing:

> *April 5, 2011: Today I feel embarrassed and a bit ashamed for having a sexual issue of my own. Counseling couples is some of the most fulfilling work I have done in the counseling field. I have seen, first-hand, couples experience greater physical and emotional healing. I have witnessed couples who haven't been physically intimate in years, due to buried hurts and resentments, begin to reach out to each other sexually. It is both humbling and honoring to know that God has used me in my clients' lives. In my head I know the truth that therapists are human and don't have to be perfect. But it's a truth my heart is struggling to grasp. God, please bring your redemption in my own life. Bring me the healing I need. A phrase from graduate school is on my mind: "We can only take clients as far as we've been willing to go ourselves."*
>
> *Lord, would You speak to me regarding my sexual vulnerabilities and struggles? Reveal Your acceptance of me, even in this place where I feel stuck. I have to believe that*

someday when I sit with couples again, I will be grateful for vaginismus and my new depth of understanding and compassion around sexual struggles.

May 10, 2011: Tonight, Stephen and I are writing this book together in our bedroom. I am reminded of how safe I feel married to a man full of integrity. He is a man who embodies God's loving-kindness. I know the enemy will do everything he can to keep Stephen and me from becoming one in body, soul, and spirit. But I also know that Christ is victorious, and Christ's plan is that Stephen and I become one. I pray that Jesus would come and fight for us and intervene on our behalf. "God, please silence the loud lies of the enemy and move us forward. Lord, please bring freedom to us and to those reading this who also have sexual struggles."

May 15, 2011: Yesterday was a doozy. On our way to a marriage conference that we're attending this weekend, I shared my sexual history with Stephen—all of it. Many of the details I had never shared with him before we got married. Stephen is understandably hurt, angry, and disappointed for the ways I didn't save myself sexually. I feel like I failed him even before meeting him. I don't feel worthy of writing this book now. After all, did I really save myself for marriage? I'm questioning this because today I learned that many women who think they are virgins are often just "technically virgins." This is because when arousal happens and oxytocin is released between two people, bonding and "oneness" happens.

This new information makes me realize I have had "oneness" moments with other men. This leaves me feeling extremely sad. But, on the encouraging side, it means that Stephen and I have consummated our marriage. Even though we haven't had intercourse, the reality is we have experienced "oneness."

Sadly, most of my bad judgment moments with guys happened because I had consumed too much alcohol and wasn't able to think clearly and make wise decisions. Also, because I didn't have my first official boyfriend until I was twenty-three years old, it was like I needed to make up for lost time. I had to now squeeze in as much dating experience as I could. When I hit thirty, my heart hardened a bit toward God. If God wasn't going to bring me a godly mate, then I decided I'd date whoever I wanted to. And so I dated whoever I was attracted to, even if it was just a physical attraction. This led me to dating a string of men who didn't love Jesus. One was an atheist. I clearly remember the night this particular boyfriend looked at me and shocked me as he said, "Rebecca, I think you're angry at God." How true he was. I was so angry at Jesus! I now see that trying to shut God out was not the answer.

Stephen was much more respectful of women he dated than I was of the men I have dated. I feel unworthy of Stephen. It hurts to know that the love of my life is struggling to respect and forgive me. I let him down, and now I feel rejected by him.

Last night, I felt God's love and acceptance, even though I wasn't feeling those things from Stephen. As I was trying to be kind to myself, self-soothe, and remember God's promise to never leave me, Stephen reached out to me in bed. He asked me if I was still awake. He then, through his words and touch, offered me his love and forgiveness. That night, I prayed that we would be able to honestly grieve our past mistakes and then be able to truly receive God's forgiveness. I want to believe the truth that I am worthy of all good gifts from God and Stephen.

Stephen and I did not honor God in all our dating relationships and decisions. We were in need of God's grace. The truth is we are all in need of God's grace. It is never too late to confess our pain and wrongdoing, receive God's amazing forgiveness, and then begin walking in a direction of purity. Even though I have made mistakes in the past, today is a new day.

> *May 23, 2011: Today I am feeling like a failure again. But this time, for not being able to have sex with my husband. Lord, I feel like You're saying there's time, it'll come; but I feel angry hearing this. Haven't we waited long enough?*
>
> *June 12, 2011: My prayer is that our story would bless future generations to come. I hope that our story would be used in others' lives to start honest conversations about the joys and struggles of their sexuality and relationships.*
>
> *June 15, 2011: I got a phone message from a close friend tonight. She reminded me that there's great joy in our love story. God delights in it. After all, He is our Father and He authored our story!*

June 24, 2011: Today was full of more personal healing and freedom. I'm forgiven for the ways I've looked outside of God for escape. I confess the times I said no to having sex but was operating in my own strength and self-righteousness. Also, God saw the event of sexual abuse that I experienced as a seven-year-old girl. He saw how traumatic it was to have a teenage guy, who I trusted, try to force himself on me sexually and ask me to do sexually inappropriate things with him. Even though we ultimately did not have intercourse, I was still left feeling powerless, out of control, and tainted sexually and spiritually. As a result, I dissociated. One part of my personality shut down, and another part of me worked hard to perform and be a perfectly pure sexual being. Lord, I confess all of that. Thank you for the integration You brought me today during my personal counseling session. You are protecting my sexuality, and I don't have to work hard to protect myself anymore. I feel lighter, and never again do I need to take on the heavy law of penance and try to save myself.

June 26, 2011: In counseling today, God reminded me of different times in my life where I've dreaded something bad happening to me and where I've felt out of control sexually. I was able to release how I've been negatively focused on by men. I also let go of much unbelief, feelings of incompetency, dogmatic thinking, and shame. I have believed the lie that "I'll always be broken sexually." Thank you, God, for breaking this lie and for bringing me truth. Thank you for speaking to me through Scripture, through Song of Songs 4:12, 16. I was a "garden locked up," but now I want Stephen to come and unseal me and breathe on my garden. I want my lover to "taste my choice fruits." I offer Stephen a pure garden yet to be discovered. Like the Shulamite in this Scripture passage, I want to be responsive, adventurous, uninhibited, expressive, and sensuous.

Thank you, God, for giving me such a safe and kind husband. My vulnerability and desire to invite Stephen in is beautiful to You, Lord. Jesus, You are worshiped as Stephen and I are united, and You will bless us with all the glories of true intimacy. Lord, please open me up to my husband.

June 28, 2011: As I brainstorm title ideas for this book, it feels like a step of faith, because right now we still haven't been able to have sex. At this point, can I honestly say that sex was well worth the wait? Deep in my heart, though, the truth is planted. The truth is we will be able to make love. It's where Christ is taking us. I want to trust that God will always continue to pour out His faithfulness upon us.

July 5, 2011: Today Stephen prayed that this would be the year that the Lord opens and blesses my womb.

July 10, 2011: As I worked through the workbook that the Carters have written about my sexual disorder, vaginismus, I felt God guiding, comforting, and giving me His courage. Christ is victorious. Today I was one step closer to making love with my husband.

July 13, 2011: I am overcome by the love that I have for Stephen. Last night he said that I add spice to his life. I see this as being true. He went on to say that he adds stability to my life; also, very true. We are a wonderful team. Even how we work together to clean up after our dinner meal, or our intimate prayer times together in the morning or before bed, shows me that we were meant to be united in a lifelong partnership. We are intimate allies, working to build God's kingdom together. Lord, thank you for blessing me with Stephen.

Thank you that you kept us unmarried until finally meeting each other. (I think Stephen's decade-long commitment to wearing a pair of dorky glasses, with huge round circles that covered most of his face, helped keep his good looks hidden from the ladies.)

August 16, 2011: It feels good to be moving forward. Today as I read through Luke chapter 1 in the Bible, I felt like God spoke to me that I, too, was to bear a son. I wonder how this is possible as I still have not been able to have intercourse with Stephen. As I waited on God to speak, I believe the Lord showed me that as He did with Mary, it will come about because of the healing power and touch of the Holy Spirit. I heard God say, "I am opening you up; nothing is impossible for Me."

September 8, 2011: The vaginismus protocol has not been easy to work through. I have cried many tears, felt stuck, and felt like giving up on numerous occasions. Some days I have had more success and growth than others. A dear friend early on offered to journey with me through my vaginismus struggles. I have sent her a text message each day before I work on the vaginismus protocol. It's made a huge difference knowing that she is cheering me on and that daily she is praying I move forward. Today she encouraged me with these words: "Each step has been a challenge, but as you have pressed on, Jesus has given you more and more victory."

September 10, 2011: Sometimes I get angry that following God isn't easier. I often want a proven formula to adhere to such as "Follow God and you'll get a happy and easy life." Or "Say yes to God's guidelines by waiting to have sex, and you'll get to live in bliss for all your days." However, in this world, the Lord promises that we will experience great joy and great sorrow. This world is not our ultimate home. The earth is full of much beauty, but also much sin, evil, and brokenness.

September 12, 2011: What has really helped is that now Stephen and I don't just see vaginismus as my condition. We now see it as our condition. As I work on going through the protocol in the vaginismus workbook, Stephen now stands outside the bathroom door to pray and envision Christ's blood over the doorpost. He meditates on the truth that by Christ's wounds I am healed.

September 16, 2011: I am extremely grateful for my stepmom. She is a gifted Christian sex therapist, and she's been an invaluable resource for us during this difficult season. I have talked through my questions and fears with her on numerous occasions. She has been compassionate and knowledgeable, offering me sound advice. I have left our conversations more hopeful.

September 29, 2011: Today Stephen and I had our greatest victory. I was able to receive my husband inside of me and enjoy making love with him. As he entered me, there was enjoyment for us both. Hallelujah! I was able to not just tell Stephen how much I loved him but also show him with my body that I trust and respect him. At last the two shall be one in every way! Thank you for relaxing me, Lord, and for allowing us to experience such wonderful intimacy. Thank you, Lord, for Your faithfulness. Thank you, Jesus, for all the times of deep physical intimacy, connection, and joy that you have in store for Stephen and me!

October 12, 2011: Today I was reminded that in my family, there has been much sexual sin. My parents never sexually abused us kids.

However, in generations before them there was much sexual molestation and abuse, sexual addictions, promiscuity, affairs, and divorce. I felt like a hypocrite today writing a book about sexual purity when I come from a family line full of child abusers and adulterers.

This afternoon, a dear friend prayed that Jesus would break a generational curse in my life regarding sexual sin. We prayed that I would no longer believe that I'm unworthy to write this book because of my sexual sins and regrets and those sins of my ancestors. We asked that God would restore blessings of sexual purity and self-control to me and my bloodline. I additionally prayed that God would restore sexual purity and self-control to you, the reader, and your bloodline as well.

October 15, 2011: At a recent leadership development conference, I was asked in a nutshell what our book was going to be about. I immediately responded, "God's faithfulness." The leader asked, "And do people need to hear about God's faithfulness?"

With tears in my eyes I answered, "Yes!" We all need to be reminded that even when we feel stuck and hopeless, God is faithful to show us the path of life that He would have us walk down. I want to get to the place where it's more important to say yes to God's call on my life and His invitations for me than it is to play it safe. I am thankful that out of Jesus' kind and loving heart, He united Stephen and me in every way—body, soul, and spirit. We are now getting to explore all that sex can be, and I'm grateful that God will lead us. God is the great Healer, and He will continue to be committed to our healing and growth.

Stephen Reflects:

Looking back now as I write this, almost seven months into our marriage, I do see signs of God's provision for us. The biggest provision was having Rebecca's dad and stepmother as a valuable resource. I imagine that there are not many people who have even one Christian sex therapist in their immediate family—we had two! They have helped many people with sexual disorders, including vaginismus. Rebecca's stepmom guided her through a protocol that is effective in overcoming this disorder. With God's help, her family's guidance, and Rebecca's diligence and persistence, we finally had victory. Six months after our wedding day, Rebecca and I officially consummated our marriage!

To celebrate our sexual union, we planned a weekend getaway to Ouray, Colorado. Ouray is called the little Switzerland of America. It is a stunning town, located in the heart of the Colorado Rockies. We enjoyed our stay at a very comfortable and romantic bed-and-breakfast. The highlights were the stunning mountain vistas, eating filet mignon at the famous Bon Ton restaurant, and hiking six miles along the perimeter trail. Other memories created were soaking in the natural hot springs and relaxing with my beautiful wife; but best of all was being able to fully enjoy my wife's body.

As Rebecca and I have reflected on the struggle we had with vaginismus, we are now able to see this problem as a gift from God. It allowed us to bond in a deeper way. This was a pathway for us to talk about our sexuality in depth with each other. We became completely honest about our sexual frustrations, our unmet expectations, and our hopes for what our sexual union could look like. We believe that we have gotten to levels of connection that take years for many couples to reach—if ever.

For Reflection:

1. What about you? Has God allowed a physical problem or obstacle in your life? The author of *Passion and Purity*, Elizabeth Elliot, used to say, "Offer it [whatever problem] to God and let it be your gateway to joy!"
2. Ask God if there are any sexual struggles or sin in your life or in your family line. Confess it to God and receive His forgiveness.
3. As you read this book, do you sense God calling you to walk in a direction of purity and submit your sexuality to His authority and design? If so, we encourage you to share with a pastor, counselor, or close friend your new commitment.

CHAPTER 18

His name means "gift from God"

Stephen Reflects:

In November 2011, Rebecca shared with me and one of our friends that she had been crying most of the day and was feeling emotional. She also had been having an upset stomach all week and thought maybe she was coming down with something. With a gleam in her eye, the friend announced, "Girlfriend, you are *so* pregnant!" Later that night, Rebecca and I went to the grocery store to purchase a couple of pregnancy tests. And, yes, they came back positive! We are looking forward, with joy, to the birth of our firstborn.

Rebecca Reflects:

Dear Baby,

Daddy and I found out that you were growing inside Mommy's tummy ten days ago. We were both thrilled to learn you existed! It felt like the most unbelievably good news in the whole world. Mommy and Daddy had to go through much healing to get pregnant. Plus, Mommy is a little bit older than some other mommies and was starting to wonder if she would be able to get pregnant. Getting to be your mommy feels like the best gift ever. It is such a wonderful miracle to have finally met your daddy and to now be waiting for your arrival. Your daddy took a picture of all three of the pregnancy tests we took. At this rate you are going to be one photographed baby!

Your expected birthday is July 15th, one day after my own birthday. Everyone is thrilled for us. Your Grammy Jany just kept saying, "My baby's having a baby." Your Uncle Jared told your daddy to start reading the Bible over you, so you could get to know his voice. Your Uncle Joshy is encouraging me to drink lots of fruit and veggie juices. Everyone is praying for your health and well-being. Your Grandpa Bill can't wait to paint your new room. Right now I'm thinking about going with a beach theme. Your Grandma Janean bought me essential oils to put on my belly. I have been tired and felt nauseous, but it's getting a bit better. It's all worth it. And, not feeling well gives me an opportunity to depend on God more and receive your daddy's help. Your daddy has such a kind servant's heart, and he's a great cook on nights I'm too sick to cook.

About three weekends ago, we visited a church where the pastor and elders were inviting folks to come forward to be prayed over and anointed with oil. I felt prompted to go forward and have the pastor pray over my womb. It was a beautiful time for your dad and me. The pastor boldly prayed we'd be pregnant within the month. He encouraged us, even if we didn't permanently land at his church, to come tell him when we were pregnant so he could rejoice with us. It will be fun to tell him our good news. It's amazing how many people have been praying for you already!

Your daddy and I have been educating ourselves about the different options regarding birth. Deep in our hearts, we knew you were coming. A few weekends ago, before we even knew you were real, we went to a film festival all about birth. Your daddy was one of the only guys that lasted all day. After doing research and watching documentaries like, "The Business of Being Born," we're hearing the invitation to have you at home with a wonderfully warm and experienced midwife.

I can't wait to reach out and kiss your sweet little cheeks and cradle you in my arms. As an act of faith and in preparation, before we were pregnant, we had already bought a La-Z-Boy rocker recliner that will be perfect for nursing and singing you sweet lullabies. Several months back, I also bought you a little outfit that says "Rock Star" on it. You are going to look great in it.

I want you to know that you have already brought Daddy and me, and our families and friends, great joy. We keep catching ourselves saying, "We're gonna have a baby!" Daddy loves to sing to you and put his hands on my belly. It's his way of reaching out and being close to you. Last night, your dad and I thanked God for blessing our union. We prayed that our experience of birth would be full of awe, wonder, and joy. I also want you to know that you were made in love. Your daddy and I love, appreciate, and enjoy each other deeply. We think that you were conceived on our second honeymoon in Ouray, Colorado.

My prayer, precious baby, is that you would always believe the truth that you are deeply wanted and loved.

Love, Mommy

Stephen Reflects:

About a month after we found out we were pregnant, I went on a spiritual retreat in the Rocky Mountains with some of my friends. It was a camp designed to help men hear God's voice. The leaders would send us out as a group and/or individually to listen for God's voice. At one point, I went for a walk alone along a mountainous dirt road. The stunning landscape, covered in pure white snow, was breathtaking. As I walked, breathing in the cool, crisp mountain air, I talked to God about things just like I would talk to a friend. It was during this time that I heard God speak: "Stephen, I love you. Stephen, you are going to have a son. He is going to help bring more healing to you."

I replied, "God, please don't put that pressure on him of [bringing more healing to me]."

God immediately responded, "Relax, son, it is going to be okay."

Later that night, I excitedly shared this information with my friends.

I was very careful with whom I shared this information, because some people think you're delusional if you say, "I heard God speak to me." To be honest, I was a bit skeptical myself. I do believe that God speaks to us and longs to have an intimate relationship with each of us, but at times I questioned whether I actually heard God speak this to me. I guess God was growing my faith in Him and in my ability to hear Him correctly. So, when our boy was born eight months later, I was full of joy, not only because of our son, but also because it confirmed to me yet again that God loves to speak to us.

Rebecca Reflects:

Dear Baby,

Active labor started around five in the evening on Thursday, July 19, 2012, and went about twelve hours. Precious baby, you were born at 5:15 a.m. on Friday, July 20, 2012. You and Mommy share the same birth month. Our doula (labor coach) was wonderful. She came over to our home at 4:00 p.m. on Thursday, and she and I took some walks through the neighborhood, while Daddy and my mom, your Grammy, did last-minute tidying up to get the house all ready for your arrival. Grammy made us all delicious chicken tacos for dinner. Strong sensations of labor kept coming, and our doula decided to stay. Eventually, our midwife and her two assistants arrived. Our birth team had been prayerfully selected, and they all were very supportive and encouraging.

Everyone present believed that God created my body to be able to give birth, and that Christ would give me the strength I needed. On the door frames throughout our home, I had posted positive affirmations, Scriptures, poems, and visualizations that I had been focusing on during pregnancy. Things like, "I can do all this through him who gives me strength" (Philippians 4:13). "My perineum and whole body are open and relaxed." "I am connected to all mothers—past, present, and future." Also, the red roses Daddy had bought for my thirty-seventh birthday, three days earlier, were a beautiful focus point for me to look at during labor. I love being married to your father. He was loving, gentle, and supportive to me during labor and birth. He was constantly by my side, cheering me on.

Labor was long and intense. It was the hardest work I'd ever done. It was tempting to try to escape the pain and run from it, but I am proud of myself for all the contractions that I surrendered to and embraced. Our doula really helped me stay present and breathe into the strong sensations I was having. It helped to be reminded that each contraction was a good thing because it was taking me one step closer to meeting you, our precious baby. It was wonderful laboring at home because I felt safe there. Our home is a refuge of peace and rest for me. The best part about being at home was that not once did I feel rushed to hurry up or do things a certain way. I got to be myself and let things unfold naturally.

My favorite moment happened sometime in the early morning hours. Daddy, our doula, Grammy, and I were all lounging on our comfortable brown couch. Even though the sensations were strong and painful, God's grace and unconditional love was being poured out upon me. Our doula commented that she strongly felt the presence of the Holy Spirit. Yes, indeed, God's peaceful and loving presence was with us, and I lifted my hands to heaven and began praying and worshiping God. It was a sacred moment for all of us. I felt so connected to the Lord and supported by our labor team. I was not alone.

Laboring through the night was tiring, but the advantage was it was cooler. It had been in the high nineties that month. The atmosphere was peaceful and cozy. We had lavender-scented candles burning and soft, relaxing, instrumental music playing. Daddy and everyone present kept telling me how proud they were of me. God kept me calm, even when your heart rate dropped a bit and we had to get out of the birth tank.

I had hoped to birth you in the water with gentle and spontaneous pushes. Daddy had trained to be right there to catch you. Instead, your daddy was needed to hold me from behind as our midwife performed an episiotomy on our living room couch. She then asked me to dig deep. With just a few strong, warrior-like, loud, guttural pushes, you were born. Within a minute, you were alert and inquisitively looking around. With joy, Daddy proudly announced, "We have a son!"

We were so happy to have a son! Indeed, we had heard the Lord's voice. I am grateful that even though the last hour of your birth was different and more intense than I had hoped for, God gave me the peace and strength I needed. The Lord kept me focused and breathing deep breaths, and He kept us both safe and healthy. You were loved immediately, and it was so special to finally get to see you face to face. At birth, I felt you looked a lot like Daddy.

You weighed seven pounds, fourteen ounces and were twenty-one inches long. We hugged you, and I felt extremely relieved and proud of myself. I was in awe of how precious you were. You were hungry from the beginning. You definitely have your parents' big appetite!

> *Within the first hour, I was able to breastfeed and give you the nourishment you needed. What a joy that I got to birth you into this world! I am so grateful to Jesus! I am honored and delighted to be your Mommy. We are going to have many wonderful adventures together!*
>
> *Love,*
> *Mommy*

To close, here are some words that members of our birth team wrote to us:

> *Rebecca and Stephen, your labor was beautiful and peaceful and looked like everything you wanted and planned for it to be. Rebecca, I loved watching your midwife and mom attending to you. You kept your sense of humor throughout and your sweet temperament. Stephen, your gentle support was perfect.*

> *First I must start with saying it was such a privilege and blessing to be with you during your birth experience! You worked so well with your labor, Rebecca! What a beautiful labor you had. Throughout the night, you moved from your bedroom, to the living room, to the bathroom. You swayed, you danced, you kneeled, and you squatted. You were quiet, you moaned, you chatted, but what I remember*

most and will hold in my heart forever is that you praised! Several times you would use your prayer language, which was so beautiful. You would raise your hands in praise, and would always give open verbal thanks to God, even when things were tough. Stephen was so sweet and gentle with you—ever encouraging. I will never forget him singing to you, and how it truly did quiet you and center you. Toward early morning you were close enough to pushing that you were able to get in the tub. . . . Even though things were more intense with the oxygen on you and the rushed atmosphere, there was still peace there. With much work from you and a wonderful team, your sweet son entered this world! The time you spent afterward bonding, nursing, and praising was so special to watch! The work wasn't over for you, though, as a very extensive repair needed to be done. But again, you and Stephen never ceased to have praise on your lips and love for each other.

Dear Son,

You are now two weeks old. We love and accept you with all our hearts, and we think you are the cutest little boy ever! Already, we are grateful for how passionate, strong, expressive, alert, smiley, and curious you are. One of our favorite things to do with you is dance around in our living room and sing worship and old camp songs over you. You are indeed God's precious gift to us!

Love,

Mommy

I am grateful that Stephen and my mom were by my side every moment through the birth of our son. As a junior high girl, I rebelled against being close with my mom, but now in my late thirties I felt so bonded with her that I wanted her to be a part of my birth team. And I was following in her footsteps by having natural births. I thank the Lord often for the restored relationship I now have with my mom. She teaches me about the joy and centering that comes from being still in God's presence. She also models the importance of nurturing my family by creating a loving and cozy home, cooking delicious meals, and making holidays, even the little ones, extra special. She currently lives in the same town as us. When she and my boys are together there are hugs, smiles, and squeals of delight as they ride slides together at the park, or sing and dance to their favorite songs. She helps them discover how fun it is to do new things, like help Mommy cook, or help Grammy water the flowers in the garden. She's always told me that being a mom to me and my brothers is her greatest joy. I'm grateful that we now get to share the joyful, and sometimes exhausting, moments of motherhood together.

Stephen Reflects:

Rebecca and I took seriously the task of naming our baby. We spent time praying about what name God had for him. God lead us to the name Matteo for our son. Matteo is the Italian version of Matthew, and it means "gift from God." I am half Italian, so I was proud to honor my heritage. Matteo's middle name is "David." We chose this name in honor of my older brother, David. He named his first-born Luke Stephen in honor of me.

David is also Rebecca's brother Josh's middle name, and "Matthew is her brother Jared's middle name. Thus, we were proud to honor all our brothers and our family heritage.

For Reflection:

1. If you have kids, take time to write about what they mean to you.
2. If you have never written down your child's birth story, take time to reflect and record highlights. If you have never told your child about their birth story, ask God if there would be anything He would have you share with them.
3. If you hope to be a parent some day, bring this desire to God now. Ask God if He is inviting you to take a step of faith as a way to anticipate your child's future arrival.

CHAPTER 19

Sex is fun and pleasurable

Rebecca Reflects:

We are in awe of God for the ways He prepared us for each other and then guided us together. God created us to be united in body, soul, and spirit. The reality, however, is our sexual relationship is just beginning. Some days it feels like it's off to a slow start. We're now two years into our marriage, and while we are now having sex, we've had lots of starts and stops. This is due to a variety of factors such as lingering issues with vaginismus, morning sickness (and, in turn, lack of sexual desire), other pregnancy discomforts, and sleep deprivation from being new parents. Also, God has recently highlighted a lie that I believed. This lie, *sex will always be hard work* kept me disconnected from my husband. I'm thankful that I have renounced this lie. It came from the pit of hell, as all lies do. Jesus is now empowering me to believe and experience the truth: *sex is fun and pleasurable.*

But believing and living in the truth is a daily challenge. Some days it feels easier to believe the lies, because they seem truer and I have data to back them up. Last night we attempted to make love and it didn't go well. I felt shut down and tired. I love Stephen deeply, but I felt no physical passion or desire to have intercourse. The fact that sex has often felt uncomfortable keeps me from wanting to keep at it. Stephen was fearful of hurting me and didn't want me to do something that I wasn't enjoying. We were left feeling discouraged, again. It's easy to think, *What's wrong with us? Why can't we get this?*

In the movies sex always seems to look so effortless. Hollywood rarely, if ever, shows a man losing his erection, crying babies in the next room, or fights that happen right before you're trying to make love. Stephen and I are still finding our flow. Many nights we feel connected and enjoy each other deeply. But sometimes it's hard to get the timing right. We're both still learning what brings us pleasure and how to ask for what we want. I want it to be easier. There are days we're still tempted to whine to God and say, "We followed You; why aren't You helping us more?" It's tempting to demand Jesus to make my life conflict free and always happy. He's the God of the universe and sometimes I treat Him like He's nothing more than a magical genie in a bottle, ready to grant my every wish. I get deceived into thinking that since God doesn't "snap His fingers" and make all our sexual pain and discomforts go away, then He must not care.

In the midst of my complaining, God continues to cut through my doubts and communicate to us that He is for our marriage. Jesus Christ is more concerned with my transformation than He is with my having a good and happy time in life. This is a hard truth to digest, and I'm not a big fan. But deep in my heart I know it to be true. When I experience deeper healing and growth, it leads to deeper peace and contentment. So, ultimately my joy and happiness are a priority to God. It's just that He knows the most loving way to get me to experience lasting joy and well-being.

In our dating life Stephen and I were challenged to trust that God is good and that He knows what's best for us. Now, in our married life, specifically in our sex life, we're also challenged to continue to believe that God is good and that He loves us. Even though we didn't have intercourse last night, it was still an intimate time of physical connection and honest conversations. At one point I said, "At this point in our marriage, I just want to be consistently enjoying sex. Soon we're going to be speaking about the benefits and blessings of waiting till marriage, and we're only just starting to experience some of these blessings. Are we frauds because we're still having sexual struggles?" As Stephen and I pondered my question, we were still convinced that it was worth it to wait with God for each other.

Since we waited for each other, we get to, now as a team, grow and discover all that God has for us. We're excited for the continued exploration and enjoyment that awaits us. Paula Rinehart reminds us in her wonderful book *Sex and the Soul of a Woman* that the pleasure we bring each other honors God.[11] Sexual union is God's idea, it is His beautiful gift to us, and He is the One protecting our marriage bed. Our sexual relationship is now within the protection of a committed and trusting marriage.

As licensed professional counselors, we have seen the devastating results of premarital sex in some of our clients. We are grateful to Jesus that He empowered us to come to marriage without diseases, comparisons, traumatic flashbacks, and paralyzing guilt and shame. We are thrilled that there has been no door for jealousy or mistrust to creep in. We have respect for each other because we didn't cross sexual boundaries during our dating life. This gives us greater confidence that sexual boundaries won't be crossed in the future.

Our virginity was a gift we gave each other. It demonstrated patience and self-control that God so graciously gave to us. It revealed that we were trustworthy and full of respect for each other's body, as well as our own. We have no soul ties with former sexual partners, and this has freed us to give ourselves entirely to each other. Our marriage bed is not crowded; we get to focus all of our attention and desire on each other.

Having many years of singleness also gave us time to develop intimate relationships with our Savior. We both have learned to look to the Lord to give us our significance and our identity. Even though we are still in need of healing, we praise God for the foundation of innocence, honesty, freedom, and playfulness that God has formed in our marriage.

We pray God's healing, freedom, and courage over you as you wait with God for the good gifts He has in store for you.

In Christ's Love,
Stephen & Rebecca

For Reflection:

1. If you are a virgin, or a recommitted virgin (it's never too late to ask for forgiveness and begin anew), share about what it's like to carry this identity.
2. If you're married and having sexual struggles, share your disappointments with God. Ask Him to reveal any lies you have believed about your marriage and your sex life, and ask Him to write His truth on your heart.
3. If you're married, take time to share with your spouse what you enjoy about your sexual relationship and what you'd love to see more of.
4. Ask God to reveal any invitations He has for you as a result of having read our love story.

Epilogue: Invitations

Stephen and I have found great hope, purpose, and peace in having a personal relationship with God. Do you have a personal relationship with Jesus Christ? If not, would you like to?

We invite you to receive God's free gift of salvation by praying the following prayer of commitment:

> *Father God, I was created to experience a loving and intimate relationship with You and with others. I acknowledge that I have been living for myself, looking for life and wholeness outside of You. I have been spiritually dead and disconnected from You, God. I am unable to meet my deepest needs. Jesus, thank you for dying on the cross for my sins and for rising again in order to buy me from slavery and give me abundant life—now, and forevermore. I repent of all my wrongdoings and my rebellion against Your authority. Jesus, You are now my Savior, and I receive Your forgiveness, grace, and new life. Holy Spirit, thank you for coming into my life and making me a new creation. Amen.*

Contact Us

Please contact us if you would be interested in having us come and speak at your church's high school, college, or young adult group.

Feel free to visit our website:
www.stephenandrebeccanthony.com

Vaginismus Resources:

If you, or someone you know, have never been able to consummate your marriage and/or have painful intercourse, I highly recommend the Carters' excellent book and workbook. It is entitled *Completely Overcome Vaginismus: The Practical Approach to Pain-Free Intercourse.* This wonderful book also gives you access to a supportive website for couples struggling with vaginismus.

End Notes

Chapter 1: Why am I waiting?
[1] McDowell, Josh, *Why Wait?: What You Need to Know about the Teen Sexuality Crisis* (Here's Life Publishers, Inc. 1987).

Chapter 2: Something is missing.
[2] C.S. Lewis, *The Four Loves* (New York: Harcourt Brace & Company, 1960), 169.

Chapter 4: I will be dating my future husband by my 35th birthday.
[3] Katherine Woodward Thomas, *Calling in "The One": 7 Weeks to Attract the Love of your Life* (New York: Three Rivers Press, 2004).
[4] Sapphire Leadership Group. Formerly Plumbline Ministries. I do not have the exact title of the talks I listened to. They are currently not listed on their website.

Ch. 16: Yea baby, that's what I'm talking about.
[5] Mark & Lisa Carter. *Completely Overcome Vaginismus: The practical approach to pain-free intercourse.* (Canada, 2002), 19.
[6] Ibid., 24, 25.
[7] Ibid., 14.
[8] Yancey, Philip. *Disappointment with God: Three Questions No One Asks Aloud* (Grand Rapids, MI: Zondervan Publishing House, 2004), 53.
[9] Jenell Williams Paris, *The End of Sexual Identity: Why Sex Is Too Important to Define Who We Are* (Downer's Grove, IL: InterVarsity Press, 2011), 12.

Ch. 17: Nothing is impossible for me.
[10] Eldredge, John & Staci. *Love and War: Find Your Way to Something Beautiful in Your Marriage* (Colorado Springs, CO: WaterBrook Press, 2009), 13.

Ch. 19: Sex is fun and pleasurable.
[11] Paula Rhinehart. *Sex and the Soul of a Woman: How God Restores the Beauty of Relationships from the Pain of Regret* (Grand Rapids, MI: Zondervan, 2004).

www.ingramcontent.com/pod-product-compliance
Lightning Source LLC
Chambersburg PA
CBHW071312110426
42743CB00042B/1320